The
Servant
Who
Rules

Discovery Books

The Servant Who Rules

Ray C. Stedman

Word Books, Publisher
Waco, Texas

Quotations from the Revised Standard Version of the
Bible, copyrighted 1946, 1952, © 1971, 1973
by the Division of Christian Education of the National
Council of the Churches of Christ in the United States
of America, are reprinted by permission.

Discovery Books are published by Word Books,
Publisher in cooperation with Discovery Foundation,
Palo Alto, California.

ISBN 0–87680–841–0
Library of Congress catalog card number: 76–20967
Printed in the United States of America

Contents

1

The Place to Begin

After spending two weeks in Mexico recently with the Wycliffe Bible Translators, I realized anew that the Gospel of Mark is the most translated book in all the world. No other book appears in as many languages. Almost all Wycliffe translators, after they have reduced a language to writing, begin their translation of the Scriptures with this Gospel. I am sure the fact that it is the shortest of the Gospels has something to do with that decision; Bible translators are human beings like the rest of us, and no one wants to start with a Gospel as long as Matthew or Luke.

But it is also a fact that Mark is particularly suitable for introducing people of all backgrounds, classes, and tribes to the Scriptures. It is the one Gospel of the four which is aimed at the gentile ear. No one can read the Gospel of Matthew without seeing that it is written for the Jew. It has to do with the Old Testament and with Jewish customs. But Mark was written for the Roman world, for the gentile, for those who do not know the background of the Old Testament. Therefore, it is a very instructive and helpful Gospel to use in the initial approach.

Many scholars think that the Gospel of Mark is the very earliest New Testament Scripture we have. It was probably written sometime in the sixties of the first century, which would make it very early, going back to the beginnings of the Christian story. Scholars differ, however, as to whether Matthew or Mark wrote first because it is hard to tell who borrowed from whom—Matthew from Mark or Mark from Matthew. We know for certain that Luke borrowed from both Matthew and Mark. It is also true that Mark's Gospel is reproduced entirely in Matthew and Luke except for a few verses. So somebody had to borrow from somebody else. Someone had someone else's account before him as he wrote.

not necessarily when God breathed the Word —

We do know that this Gospel was written by a young man named John Mark, who appears several times in our Scriptures. His mother, whose name was Mary, was a rather wealthy woman who had a big house in Jerusalem. In the twelfth chapter of Acts we are told that the early disciples met in her house for a large church prayer meeting for Peter when he was put in prison. We know that young John Mark was taken by Paul and Barnabas on their first missionary journey and traveled with them to the island of Cyprus. But for some reason— we are never told quite why—Mark refused to go with them when they went on into the mainland of what is now Turkey. Instead he went back home to his mother's house. Paul was upset about that and evidently felt that Mark was a quitter.

When it came time for them to go out again, although Barnabas wanted to bring Mark, Paul would not let him come. So they separated. Barnabas took Mark with him to Cyprus, and Paul and Silas went back to the areas where they had gone before. Then Mark drops out of sight for a time.

The next we hear of him, he is an associate of Peter, who speaks very affectionately of this young man, calling him "Mark, my son" in his first letter. Early church tradition tells us that Mark became the companion of Peter. Eusebius, a church father writing in the third century, says that the early Christians were so entranced with all the things Peter told them that they asked Mark to write them down. Perhaps that is how we got The Gospel According to Mark, for it reflects much of Peter's memories and experiences with Jesus.

This much about the origin of the Gospel of Mark can be verified from Scripture. But there is another aspect of it which perhaps I ought to call "Stedman's speculation"; it is not inspired, but it has long intrigued me. In Mark 14:51, reference is made to an incident which only Mark records. In his account of Jesus' betrayal and arrest, Mark tells us that as Jesus was being led away by the soldiers, a young man followed him who was wearing nothing but a linen cloth. Apparently thinking that he was a disciple of Jesus who had been foolish enough to remain behind while all the others had run for their lives, the soldiers attempted to seize him. But all they got was the cloth as he ran naked into the night. Many scholars have suggested that this was Mark, for he would have been a young man at that time. Perhaps, because of his fascination with Jesus, he had been hanging around, hoping to learn more, and he fell into this trap unknowingly and had had to flee for his life. The fact that Mark is the only one who mentions this incident is highly suggestive that this indeed was Mark himself.

A Personal Note

But another fascinating story, found in Mark 10, and recorded in Matthew and Luke as well, is the story of the rich young ruler. Here we have a young man who, toward the end of Jesus' ministry, came to him with a question. He was a wealthy member of the ruling class, evidently a handsome, warmly appealing person. He ran up and knelt at Jesus' feet, and said, "Good Teacher, what must I do to inherit eternal life?" Then Jesus asked him if he kept the commandments. The young man said he had kept them from his youth. Then

Mark records something that neither of the other accounts tells us. He says, "And Jesus looking upon him loved him . . ." That little personal note suggests to me that Mark was that rich young ruler.

So perhaps that little story of the young man who ran away without his robe is Mark's way of telling us that the rich young ruler who went from Jesus so sorrowfully did not remain sad. Later on perhaps, having thought things over, he made the commitment Jesus required of him: He gave away all that he had. He gave up his inheritance, and all he had left was a robe —he lost even that, finally—and he came and followed Jesus. I do not say that the Scriptures tell us explicitly this is what happened, but I think it is! So, if you do not mind the "Stedmanac" version, this gives us a little added insight into The Gospel According to Mark.

At any rate, if something like that happened, it would account for Mark's apparent fascination with two qualities of Jesus which he gives to us in the very first words of this Gospel: "The beginning of the gospel of Jesus Christ, the Son of God." The combination of Jesus of Nazareth, a carpenter, the human Jesus, with the Son of God, the Divine One appears to have made a strong impression on Mark. In fact, the book is organized according to these two qualities of Jesus; it falls into two halves. The first, chapter 1 through chapter 8:26, is about "The Servant Who Rules"—the authority of the servant. The second, from chapter 8:27 through to the end, is "The Ruler Who Serves." Let's read the opening verses:

> The beginning of the gospel of Jesus Christ, the Son of God. As it is written in Isaiah the prophet, "Behold, I send my messenger before thy face, who shall prepare thy way; the voice of one crying in the wilderness: Prepare the way of the Lord, make his paths straight—" John the baptizer appeared in the wilderness, preaching a baptism of repentance for the forgiveness of sins. And there went out to him all the country of Judea, and all the

people of Jerusalem; and they were baptized by him in the river Jordan, confessing their sins (Mk. 1:1–5).

That is an amazing statement! Mark's emphasis right from the outset is the ministry of John the Baptist. This is what he calls "the beginning of the gospel"; it is the place to begin. And the highlight of that ministry was the fantastic success John enjoyed way out in the wilderness. Not long ago I was in that wilderness. We drove from the city of Jerusalem down to Jericho, then up the valley of the Jordan River. This is indeed a wilderness. It is a dreary, desolate, forsaken, lonely spot—even today. The Jordan flows through here, but it is the only water for miles around. It is a parched and dreary place, rimmed by barren desert mountains.

Yet the people of Jerusalem and Judea left their cities, left their recreations and pleasures, and trekked through this desolate wilderness to listen to a man preach. They probably had to walk twenty or thirty miles to hear John, but they went willingly and in such increasing crowds that Mark says in only slight exaggeration here, that "all the country of Judea, and all the people of Jerusalem" came out to hear him.

Most of us conceive of John as a rugged, fearless individual who preached thundering judgment and torment and condemnation to everybody. But if that were the kind of message John preached, nobody would have left Jerusalem to hear it. Nobody is interested in going to hear somebody excoriate them, strip and lash and flay them. Anybody who preaches like that does not have much of a following for long. John did not preach like that; Mark tells us that his message was the beginning of the good news of Jesus Christ. Something drew these people out of all these cities and brought them down into this desert area. It was to listen to this strange and rugged young preacher proclaim good news to them.

It is evident that John spoke to a universal need in their lives. We do not have to guess what it was because it is still around. It is exactly the same need that grips people's hearts today. They were victims of a syndrome that afflicts every human being today as well as then. The syndrome consists of three elements which always go together: sin, guilt, and fear.

Reaching In

What is sin? Basically and fundamentally, sin is nothing but self-centeredness. We commit sins because we are thinking of ourselves, loving ourselves, indulging ourselves, and taking care that no one gets ahead of us. That is the essence of sin— self-centeredness. We are all victims of it. There is not one of us who does not struggle in this area. We find ourselves trapped in it constantly. That is the curse which hangs over our whole human race. We were made by God to be vessels to convey his outgoing love, to reach out with it to everyone around us. Somehow that has become twisted so that now instead of reaching out we reach in, and we love ourselves first.

And sin always produces guilt. Guilt is dislike of ourselves. We do not like the fact that we hurt others—and we know we do. We feel responsible because we see the damage we do in other people's lives by our self-centeredness, and we feel guilty about it. We learn to hate ourselves to a considerable degree. That is why psychologists say that the great problem humanity wrestles with is self-hatred. Carl Menninger's book, *Man Against Himself,* documents this very struggle. We hate ourselves. We do not like ourselves. We lose our self-respect. That is guilt.

Guilt is always accompanied by fear, because fear is self-distrust. Fear is feeling unable to handle life any more, being aware that there are forces and powers we are unable to control and which eventually are going to confront us. We are not able to handle them, and so we run from them. Even in the Garden of Eden, as soon as Adam and Eve sinned, they felt guilty and hid in fear. It has been the history of the race ever since. Fear looms up—that uncertainty about the future, and we become fearful, timid people, afraid of what will happen next. We are walking on eggs all the time, afraid of being accepted or rejected, afraid of what people will do to us—and especially afraid of what God is going to do to us. That is an inner torment the like of which there is no equal.

One of the places I saw on a trip to Mexico City was the Shrine of Guadelupe. According to legend, the Virgin Mary appeared to an Indian back in the sixteenth century and healed him. Subsequently, the site has become a healing shrine to which people come from all of Mexico. There are rooms stacked with crutches, left behind by people who have thrown them away, feeling they had been healed at the shrine, as some may have been. But any day you go there you can see people walking on their knees, crawling for blocks over dirty, rough pavement to get to that shrine. It is painful. They leave bloodstains on the pavement as they crawl along. Why would they do such a thing? Because the outward torture of bloody, lacerated knees is not half so hard to bear as their inner torment of guilt and fear. Someone has told them this will relieve that inner torment, and this is why they do it.

If we think that is superstitious nonsense, we need to look at some of the means we employ to free ourselves of guilt and fear. There is philanthropy, for instance. Some people try to give their money away. I know many people who have benefited from guilty consciences, as wealthy individuals have tried to satisfy that inner sense of guilt and fear by giving money to some cause or other. Then there are those who turn into rigid moralists, who think of themselves as practically perfect, while looking down on those (everybody else) who do not measure up to the standard they have set for themselves—to which they do not measure up either. But that is a way of paying for the guilt inside—a way widely evident in evangelical circles, incidentally.

The Word Is Out!

A rumor of relief from this torment of guilt is what drove all these people out of Jerusalem. Here, suddenly, appeared a strange man who announced something. That is all he did. He never told how it worked, or why; he just announced it. But somehow the word got back to Jerusalem that it was working, that people were finding relief. The city began to stir as word spread from mouth to mouth, until finally, the people began to stream out into this desert place and find John the Baptist, listen to what he had to say, and be baptized by him. An amazing phenomenon, is it not?

Now, what was it that he announced which drew people like that? This is what Mark settles on next. He sees four things in the ministry of John. One, it was anticipated in the Old Testament; the prophets spoke of it. Two, John appeared in a wilderness, according to that promise. Three, he announced the way to God. And four, he assured people that it was true by the symbol of baptism. We will look at those individually.

First, this anticipation in the Old Testament: Mark quotes two of the prophets although he names only one. "Behold, I send my messenger before thy face, who shall prepare thy way," is from Malachi, the last book of the Old Testament. Mark does not mention him, and some scholars have gotten all upset about this, for they think Mark was mistaken and ascribed to Isaiah something written by Malachi. You can read hundreds of pages of argument on this. But Mark was not mistaken or ignorant; he simply wanted to stress what Isaiah said because what Malachi wrote agrees with it. So he simply combines the two and begins with a word from Malachi, "Behold, I, God, send my messenger before thy (Messiah's) face, who shall prepare thy way . . ." Then Isaiah comes in, ". . . the voice of one crying in the wilderness: Prepare the way of the Lord, make his paths straight—" And, in accordance with that prophecy, Mark says, "John the baptizer appeared in the wilderness, preaching a baptism of repentance for the forgiveness of sins."

Why would God have anticipated this truth so strongly? God knew that a step of preparation had to be made in the hearts of men before God and man could come together. God does not just suddenly appear before men and expect them to receive him. That would only frighten them to death. Some preparation had to be made. So John was sent as that preparer —to go before the Lord and prepare the way for him by means of repentance, which we will examine in a moment.

The Worst Possible Place

Why was it predetermined that John was to begin his ministry in the wilderness? If he had been listening to the public relations men of that day, he would never have begun in a wilderness. That is certainly no place to start a ministry with which you expect to reach the whole populace. But God seldom listens to PR men—or they to him—and so John began his ministry in the worst possible place. But it worked!

God chose the wilderness because it is a very apt symbol of where John's message was to fall—upon the wilderness of mankind. The desert is a picture of us, of our dry, empty, barren, weary, bored, and distraught lives. The other day I was reading an article on the breakup of the marriages of various well-known movie stars. In the beginning many of these pairs had been heralded as ideal couples. But then we get the inside story of what was going on. Do you know what broke up these marriages? Sheer, utter boredom. They were just bored—bored with each other, bored with their lives—having everything they ever wanted, but not wanting what they had.

A Christian friend told me about a neighbor he had known for a long time, a very intelligent man who made a lot of money and had everything he wanted. But he came over one day, sat down at my friend's kitchen table, buried his face in his hands, and said, "God, but I'm bored!" Two weeks later he took his own life. That is the desert, that is where people live. And that is why John appeared there. It is God's symbol to us of the hope that will spring up, even in the midst of the desert of our experience.

Then John announced this great word: Repentance is the way man comes to God, and the result of repentance is the forgiveness of sins. The greatest blessing a person can experience is to have his sins forgiven. This is what these people were looking for, and this is what they found as they streamed out of Jerusalem to listen to John. They found forgiveness of sins, and it came by way of repentance.

Forgiveness needs to be understood. It is always in two movements. Somehow we have grown up with the idea that you forgive people only when they come and apologize to you. If you can get the person who has done something wrong to admit it and apologize to you, then you forgive him. That is absolutely wrong! Very few acts of reconciliation would ever take place on that basis. No, forgiveness has to start before the offender comes to you.

Forgiving Is Forgetting

That is the glory of the story of the prodigal son, is it not? He came back from the far country, having wasted his father's goods and his own life, broken and humbled and ready to make himself his father's servant. But the moment his father spied him, his arms were open. And before that boy could say a word he was in his father's arms, being kissed and hugged while the fatted calf was prepared. Forgiveness starts in the heart of the one offended. He finds a basis on which, for some reason valid to him, he is ready to forget the hurt, to absorb it all himself and forget it. Because that is what forgiveness means—forgetting it, not holding it over the person's head and bringing it up every now and then, but forgetting it and treating the person as if it had never happened.

The basis on which God does that is the cross of Jesus Christ.

It renders him free to do so because it protects and maintains his justice. But the basis upon which we are exhorted to forgive is that we ourselves have already been forgiven. That is why Jesus told the story of the man who had been forgiven a tremendous debt, but who then grabbed by the throat a man who owed him ten dollars, and said, "Pay me what you owe me!" Jesus says that is what we are like when we do not forgive those who offend us. We have been forgiven a tremendous debt, and on that basis we are to forgive others. So that is where it starts—in a change of attitude in the heart of the one who has been offended.

But it can never be successful or complete until there has been a change of attitude in the heart of the offender. That is, forgiveness must be accepted by the one who has given the offense. He has to acknowledge that it was an offense, has to acknowledge the guilt. That is what is called "repentance." You must change your mind, stop justifying it, admit that it was hurtful, and then the pardon can be received, forgiveness can be applied. That is why John preached repentance—because it is the place where God meets man.

God's Bulldozer

That is why the prophet Isaiah said John's message would be like a great bulldozer, building a highway in the desert for God to come to the isolated stranger in the midst of the wilderness. Without a road you cannot drive out into the desert in order to help somebody. You must have a road, a highway in the desert. John was God's bulldozer to build that highway. You know how roads are built—exactly as Isaiah describes it:

> Every valley shall be lifted up, and every mountain and hill be made low; the uneven ground shall become level, and the rough places a plain (Isa. 40:4).

That is what repentance does. It brings down all the high peaks of pride that we stand on and refuse to admit are wrong. It takes

the depressed areas of our life, where we beat and torture and
punish ourselves, and lifts them up. It takes the crooked places,
where we have lied and deceived, and straightens them out.
And it makes the rough places plain. Then God is there at that
instant of repentance. Beautiful imagery, is it not? With this
Mark links the character of John: "Now John was clothed
with camel's hair, and had a leather girdle around his waist,
and ate locusts and wild honey" (Mk. 1:6).

Why would Mark put all that in? Here is this rugged
prophet John; he is no fashion plate with his camel's hair
clothes, leather sandals, and leather girdle around his waist—
very much like Elijah. And his diet was very simple: locusts
(grasshoppers) and wild honey. This is important or it would
not be here. Again, it is symbolic. But what does it symbolize?
Well, you cannot wear anything more fundamental in the way
of clothing or eat a more basic diet than John did. These things
—his clothes and his diet—are representative of his ministry,
one of simple beginnings. It is not the end; it is the beginning.
The beginning of the gospel of Jesus Christ, the Son of God,
is repentance on man's part. That is the place to begin. Even
John's clothing and his diet reflected that message.

His diet, by the way, was balanced. Food faddists will recognize immediately that grasshoppers are protein and honey is
carbohydrate. John's diet was in beautiful balance, so that he
was a healthy man. But it was a most elementary, rudimentary
sort of diet, just as his ministry was elementary, rudimentary,
right from the beginning. Furthermore, John himself said it
was incomplete:

> And he preached, saying, "After me comes he who is mightier
> than I, the thong of whose sandals I am not worthy to stoop
> down and untie. I have baptized you with water; but he will
> baptize you with the Holy Spirit" (Mk. 1:7–8).

John is very honest here. He says, "Don't look to me for answers beyond what I have already told you about repentance.
Anything beyond that must come from Another, who is coming

right after me. He is so much greater than I that I am not even worthy to untie his shoes. (This was his cousin he was referring to!) Although I can take you to the place of outward cleansing only, the sign of his greatness is that he can do much more." In other words, John could bring people *to* God, but he could not take them beyond that—*on with* God. That required the life of the Holy Spirit. When Jesus came, he would baptize them with the Holy Spirit so that they could continue to *live* as they had begun. So much of Christian preaching today is on the same order as John's ministry—designed only to bring people to God, and nothing more. It does not teach them how to live beyond that, and so people cannot go on. They know nothing of the power of the life of Jesus available through the Holy Spirit. For all that was to come after John.

John brought people to Christ by the only way man can come—through acknowledgment of guilt. When people come this way, God meets them, cleanses them, and forgives them. John demonstrated that by the baptism he performed. But there is a greater baptism—that of the Holy Spirit. And on the day of Pentecost, when the Spirit of God came, you find Peter standing up and offering people two things: forgiveness of sins and the promise of the Spirit. From that time on, this is what God has made available to any man or woman who will begin at the beginning—the place of repentance.

Have you ever repented? Have you ever changed your mind, stopped defending yourself and trying to blame everything on others, and said, "No, Lord, it's not they, it is just me. This is the way I am, and I need help"? That is the place God will meet you. He always meets man at that point, washes away guilt, cleanses, forgives. That is where you will find forgiveness of sins. If you have never repented before, I urge you to do so now. God will meet you right there. In the quiet of your own heart where God alone hears, you can say to him, "Lord, I repent. Lord, send me the Holy Spirit through Jesus the Lord." And he will.

If you are a Christian with a desert area in your life and you do not know how to handle it, this is the place to begin. Repent, acknowledge it, and God will meet you there and wash it all away. He does not have a word of condemnation for you, just a word of cleansing—if you meet him at that place of repentance.

2

Jesus Came

"In those days Jesus came . . ."

We are studying Mark's record of what happened when Jesus came to Israel. Those two little words, "Jesus came," are always a formula for dramatic and radical change. In the next two paragraphs in Mark 1:9–15, the phrase "Jesus came" occurs twice. In verse 9: "In those days Jesus came from Nazareth of Galilee . . ." And again in verse 14: "Now after John was arrested, Jesus came into Galilee . . ." Mark says that when Jesus came, he came in this two-fold way. Verse 9 begins the record of the baptism and temptation of Jesus. Jesus came, he was baptized, and he was tempted. Mark puts the latter two in the passive voice, i.e., they were done *to* Jesus. This indicates, therefore, something in the way of preparation for his ministry. Two things were necessary before he began: he needed to be baptized and to be tempted. After that, verse 14, he came into Galilee *preaching,* and in that one word is recorded the content of the activity which marked the entire career of Jesus: He came preaching. This will be the outline of our study. Let us look at the two acts of preparation Mark records which Jesus found necessary before beginning his ministry:

In those days Jesus came from Nazareth of Galilee and was
baptized by John in the Jordan. And when he came up out of
the water, immediately he saw the heavens opened and the
Spirit descending upon him like a dove; and a voice came from
heaven, "Thou art my beloved Son; with thee I am well
pleased" (Mk. 1:9–11).

All four Gospels record the baptism of Jesus. Therefore, it
evidently was very significant in the life of our Lord. Yet there
is something strange about this baptism. As we have seen, a
remarkable spiritual awakening had broken out in Israel. Literally thousands of people were leaving their homes, their jobs,
their families, and streaming out of the cities down into the
desert to listen to John the Baptist, who was saying things that
touched the core of the souls of people and spoke to their need.
They were coming out of the cities because they felt the torment of their guilt, their inadequacy, their lack of a sense of
acceptance before God. John was offering a way out, and they
responded in great numbers. And John baptized all who repented, acknowledged their guilt, and sought forgiveness of
sins. This was the emphasis of John's ministry. He granted
baptism as a sign of the cleansing of God only to those who
genuinely acknowledged their need before God by confessing
their sins. And there were thousands of them.

Yet when Jesus came out of Galilee to John to be baptized,
John protested. Matthew tells us that when Jesus came, John
said to him, "Why do you come to me? I have need to be
baptized by you." That is a remarkable statement, especially if
you remember that John did not know at this time that Jesus
was Messiah. In fact, the Gospel of John tells us that John the
Baptist knew this only when he saw the Spirit of God descending upon Jesus and remaining upon him, for that was the sign
God had given to him. Then he knew that this was the One who
was to come, the One he had been announcing. Now, John
had known Jesus ever since boyhood, for they were cousins.

And if you can't find fault with your relatives, whom can you find fault with? Yet it is most remarkable that when *this* relative comes, John says to him, "You don't need to be baptized. Why are you coming to me?" There was nothing in Jesus' life that John had seen which required repentance and confession of sins.

Sign of Intent

Jesus answered John in a most remarkable way, recorded in Matthew 3:15: "Let it be so now; for thus it is fitting for us to fulfil all righteousness." Why was Jesus baptized by John the Baptist? In this brief account Mark seems to suggest three things which will help us answer that question. First, Jesus' being baptized was an act of identification. Jesus was associating himself with us. He took our place, but he began with his baptism, not the cross. This was the first step leading to that relationship in which he was ultimately to be made sin for us, to actually become what we are. This was the first sign of his intention to do so—when he took the place of a sinner, and was baptized with a baptism of repentance and confession of sin.

I like the way Dr. H. A. Ironside explained this. He said that we are like paupers who have accumulated so many debts that we cannot pay them. These are our sins. These tremendous claims are made against us, and we cannot possibly meet them. But when Jesus came, he took all these mortgages and notes and agreements we could not meet and endorsed them with his own name, thereby saying that he intended to pay them; he would meet them. This is what his baptism signifies, and it is why Jesus said to John the Baptist, ". . . thus it is fitting for us to fulfil all righteousness." He declared his intention to meet the righteous demands of God by himself undertaking to pay the debts of men. So the baptism was clearly an act of identification.

But it was also, as you will note from Mark's account, an

empowering moment: "And when he came up out of the water, immediately he saw the heavens opened and the Spirit descending upon him like a dove . . ." ("Immediately" is Mark's favorite word, by the way. He uses it again and again all through this account.) It is very significant that the moment Jesus begins to take our place, the Father gives him the gift of the Holy Spirit. There is no greater gift God can give to men. There is no greater need that we have as individuals than to receive the gift of the Holy Spirit. It is by the Holy Spirit that man is able to live as he wants to live, and longs to live, and is able to overcome the power of sin and guilt and fear within us. Therefore the primary, elementary, most fundamental need of guilty men is the gift of the Holy Spirit. Thus when Jesus began to take our place, there was immediately given to him the gift of the Holy Spirit.

Now, this is not the first time Jesus "had" the Spirit—we must not think of it that way. It is recorded of John the Baptist that he was filled with the Holy Spirit from his mother's womb. And certainly if that was true of John, it was also true of Jesus. He lived by the Spirit during those quiet years in Nazareth. He submitted himself to his parents, grew up in a carpenter's shop and learned the trade. And through those uneventful days, living in ordinary circumstances in that little village, Jesus lived by the power of the Spirit in his life—there is no question about it.

Anointed with Power

Then what is happening now, when the Spirit comes upon him like a dove? The answer is that he is given a new manifestation of the Spirit, especially in terms of power. To use the language of Scripture, Jesus was "anointed" by the Spirit at this point. In Old Testament times they anointed kings and priests by pouring oil upon their heads, committing them to the function and office in which they were to serve. This is the picture of what is now occurring in Jesus' life. He is being anointed by God through the Spirit with power—power to meet the demands of the ministry upon which he is about to launch. That is why the Spirit, in this sense, is always associated with the coming of power into a life. Our Lord is anointed with power. Some weeks later, in the synagogue at Nazareth, Luke tells us, Jesus quoted a passage in Isaiah 61 which dealt with this, and applied the words to himself:

> "The Spirit of the Lord is upon me, because he has anointed me to preach good news to the poor. He has sent me to proclaim release to the captives and recovering of sight to the blind, to set at liberty those who are oppressed, to proclaim the acceptable year of the Lord" (Luke 4:18–19).

These were the ministries that were his during the next three and a half years, and now his public ministry begins with the anointing by the Holy Spirit with power.

Do not think of this as something remote from us. Remarkable as they may be, nevertheless all these things that happened to Jesus can happen, and indeed *must* happen, to us. That is the whole thrust of this teaching. He was taking *our* place, therefore, what happened to him must happen to *us*. That is why Jesus, standing with his disciples after the resurrection, said to them, "But you shall receive power when the Holy Spirit has come upon you; and you shall be my witnesses in Jerusalem and in all Judea and Samaria and to the end of the earth" (Acts 1:8). This is true. The Spirit of God must come upon us. The gift of the Holy Spirit must be given to us so that we might have the power to live as God wants us to live.

That is not so that we can perform dramatic acts, but rather so that we may have a new quality of life which is beautiful and resistless and yet quiet and gentle. Notice the symbol of the kind of power that is given here—it is a dove. Football teams sometimes use birds as emblems, signs of their power and ability. We have the Falcons and the Eagles—even the Ducks.

But did you ever hear of a team called the Doves? No, no team would ever use a dove as a symbol of its power. Jesus later emphasized the fact that doves are harmless; he said we are to be harmless as doves. But what is a dove? A dove is a gentle, nonthreatening bird, one that does not resist, does not fight back, and yet, amazingly enough, is irresistible.

This is the power that Jesus is describing—the power of love, of course—love that can be beaten and battered down and put to death and yet can rise again until it wins the day—that amazing love Jesus released. The greatest force in the world today, without a doubt, is love. And yet it is the kind of power that does not threaten or break apart or destroy; it gathers and heals. It is rejected, turned aside, and beaten down; yet it rises again and again. So the dove is an apt symbol of the new life our Lord came to teach. In the world we are taught that life is lived by the principle of the survival of the fittest. "Beat your way to the top of the heap, trample others down to achieve what you want. Might makes right, and every man for himself"—this is the philosophy of life advocated by the world.

But Jesus came to introduce another way, in fact, the *only* way that truly works. You could describe it as "the survival of the humblest." The virtue Christians must always be seeking is humbleness, humility. "If any man would be first, let him become the servant of all," said Jesus. Peter put it very precisely: "Humble yourselves therefore under the mighty hand of God, that in due time he may exalt you." Pride makes God our enemy, who works to cast us down, to overthrow us in every way he can.

The third aspect of his baptism is that it was a sign of assurance to Jesus. There came a voice from heaven: "Thou art my beloved Son, with thee I am well pleased." In Matthew it is stated a little differently: "This is my beloved Son, with whom I am well pleased." This was said as a testimony to those who were watching the scene. But Mark and Luke report that the voice said, *"Thou* art my beloved Son . . ."—as addressed to Jesus. There have been all kinds of quarrels among scholars as to which was correct; this simply indicates how little we understand of the ways of God.

Both Public and Personal

It is my belief that both are right, that those who were standing around heard the voice saying, "This is my beloved Son," as the stamp of God's approval upon the thirty years he spent in Nazareth, those quiet years of Jesus' life about which Scripture is silent. Men have wondered, "Perhaps he was just like everybody else; perhaps he sinned in the same way. Perhaps he was disobedient to his parents, got into fist-fights, maybe did even worse things—we don't know." But God knew. God the Father says, "This is my beloved Son, in whom I am *well* pleased." It was a testimony to the purity of those years.

But when Jesus heard it, it was, "Thou art my beloved Son," and was addressed to him directly as a ground of assurance and security for him. We must not think of Jesus as being automatically empowered against all obstacles and threats and fears. He was a *man*—that is what Scripture says. He was like us. He was assaulted with every pernicious threat that humans ever feel. He felt like us, and he needed to be treated as we need to be treated. He needed the assurance of the Father's recognition of who he was. Psychologists tell us that if we do not know who we are, we have little poise and confidence. We have to know who we are before we can have security in our speech and actions. This is what God has given to Jesus, the security of knowing that he is his beloved Son.

And, you know, this is exactly what he says to us. The glory of this gospel message is that God is ready to treat us exactly as he treated Jesus. We ought to say to ourselves every morning, "This is what my Father is saying to me: 'Thou art my beloved son, or daughter, in whom I am well pleased.' " That is what gives us a sense of security and identity, a place to stand, which means we can be calm and unthreatened when

everything goes to pieces around us. This is where it comes
from—no other source. That is why Jesus could begin his
ministry with this sense of assurance from his Father that all
was well in his life. Mark then brings us to the second act of
preparation, which was Jesus' temptation:

> The Spirit immediately drove him out into the wilderness. And
> he was in the wilderness forty days, tempted by Satan; and he
> was with the wild beasts; and the angels ministered to him
> (Mk. 1:12–13).

Part of the preparation of Jesus was this temptation he went
through. Both Matthew and Luke record this as well as Mark,
although John leaves it out. But it was necessary that our Lord
experience this testing. Notice the strong language Mark uses
here. His account is very brief, but it is highly suggestive. There
are three things here. First, the Spirit immediately (there is
that word again) drove him out into the wilderness. *Drove*
him. That means Jesus felt a strong inner compulsion, a powerful urge to go into the wilderness and face the tempter on his
own ground.

To Prove His Manhood

Last week I watched a group of high school boys turning out
for football practice. They were evidently a freshman team,
with young, eager faces, intent and alert, obviously interested
in what they were about to do. It took me back to the year I
first went out for football practice. I could not help but remember how I felt about it. It was something I had to do to prove
my manhood, yet I was a bit scared to try. I didn't know what
it would do to me. I remember turning out for practice that
first morning along with all the others, eager to do it, wanting
to do it, feeling I had to do it, and yet inwardly scared—but
not willing to admit all my fears. This is something of what
Jesus faced as he went into this temptation. He felt a strong

compulsion that he had to prove his manhood before he came to that ultimate encounter with the devil on the cross. He had to be tempted, had to undergo it for his own sake. He did not dare go out to a ministry while he was yet untried. In order that he might know what was in himself, what he could and could not stand, he was driven by the Spirit out to this place. This was intended to toughen him. This is what God always does with his men and women—toughens them by driving them out into these kinds of experiences. This is what happened to Jesus.

We are told that he went through a very severe and thorough testing. He was tested in the wilderness for forty days, tempted by Satan. Forty days is a long time to go without food. At times I have fasted for as long as three days and have found it quite endurable. Nevertheless, hunger increases as you go along. After awhile it disappears, only to come back in intensified form. And forty days is a long time. Just consider for a moment the things that have happened to you and in the world around you during the past month or so. Forty days ago can seem like the dim past because of all that has transpired since.

The Nature of the Tests

Mark suggests what other writers do not—that Jesus was tempted by the devil. In other words, the devil came to try him out in every possible way—body, soul, and spirit. He probed and assaulted and sifted and scrutinized and assailed him. The devil bombarded Jesus with every thought and every temptation that we human beings are subject to. When you read the other accounts, you can see that Matthew and Luke gather up the final temptations, the final mighty tests that Satan gave to Jesus. But these indicate the nature of the tests which came throughout this entire forty-day period, devised by the master tempter of all, the one who knows how to find the weakness in our hearts. He knows how to get at us and upset us.

There in the desert Jesus was tempted and pressured and

probed in every way. His physical hunger gath
experiences we have when our circumstances
How many of us have been overthrown by th
not think Jesus knew that he was going to be f
desert. He probably didn't know how long it
expected at any moment that God would supply
yet his privation went on, week after week, while he grew
weaker and weaker in body. The tempter would come and say,
"God doesn't care for you any more. He's abandoned you. You
say you're the Son of God? Why, he's made no provision for
you at all!" Finally that last subtle suggestion: "Why don't
you turn the stones into bread, if you're the Son of God?" That
is the way Satan gets at us, isn't it? Things go wrong; provision
does not come. We lose our job, are out of money, or tremendous obligations strike us. We do not have what it takes to
meet the need, and we say, "Where's God?" That was the
temptation Jesus faced.

Then the loneliness of spirit—all alone for forty days without human companionship. It made him long to prove himself
before men and gain their acceptance, even their admiration.
This culminated in the tempter's taking him to the pinnacle of
the temple and telling him to cast himself down: "Men will
follow you when they see God support you and sustain you in
this supernatural way." Jesus was sorely tempted to gain the approval of men by the exercise of power apart from the will of
God. And how we are tempted that way! There is no difference
at all.

Then the last temptation. With Jesus vulnerable, the devil
suggested that there was a way he could gain what he wanted,
a shortcut which would not involve death to himself. He
could have it without the cross. He took Jesus to a high mountain and showed him all the kingdoms of the world—what
Jesus was after—and said, "You can have it all if you fall down
and worship me." Our Lord met every temptation in the same
way that we can meet them—by simple reliance on and trust

in what God has written in his Word: "It is written . . ."
Three times he said it. In the physical, the mental, and the
spiritual areas of life, "It stands written."

Surely, God does this all the time. He is not through testing
people. His tests are designed to toughen us and strengthen
us. Let me share with you a poem I ran across:

> When God wants to drill a man,
> And thrill a man,
> And skill a man;
> When God wants to mold a man
> To play the noblest part,
> When he yearns with all his heart
> To create so great and bold a man
> That all the world shall be amazed,
> Watch his methods, watch his ways—
> How he ruthlessly perfects
> Whom he royally elects.
> How he hammers him and hurts him,
> And with mighty blows, converts him
> Into trial shapes of clay
> Which only God understands,
> While his tortured heart is crying,
> And he lifts beseeching hands.
> How he bends but never breaks
> When his good he undertakes.
> How he uses
> Whom he chooses,
> And with every purpose, fuses him,
> By every act, induces him
> To try his splendor out.
> God knows what he's about.

Yes, he does. That is what he did with Jesus to toughen him
and test him and prove him. Mark records one other thing
about Jesus' temptation. Despite the fact that he was without
human help and assailed by the tempter in all these ways,

nevertheless, he was not alone. He was sustained by a ministry of comfort which came in unusual ways; he was with the wild beasts, and the angels came and ministered to him. Jesus was not afraid of being attacked by the leopards, lions, bears, and other wild animals that were all around throughout that wilderness area. Mark says that Jesus was *with* them. They were his companions. They comforted him and helped him. I can picture Jesus, his body cold from hunger, snuggled up between two mountain lions—ministered to physically by the animals.

And further, the angels ministered to him. That means his thought-life was sustained; his inner life, his emotions were upheld, his mental faculties kept clear. That is the ministry of angels—invisible yet very real. Many of us have experienced the ministry of angels without even knowing it. Sometimes when your spirits are suddenly uplifted and you do not even know why, that is the ministry of angels. And Jesus was upheld that way. Finally, equipped by the Spirit, toughened, tested, Jesus comes into Galilee:

> Now after John was arrested, Jesus came into Galilee, preaching the gospel of God, and saying, "The time is fulfilled, and the kingdom of God is at hand; repent, and believe in the gospel" (Mk. 1:14–15).

Here Mark passes over a full year of Jesus' ministry. You have to get the details from John's Gospel, for John alone records it—his encounter with Nicodemus, the woman at the well, the wedding at Cana, etc. Mark passes over this in silence and begins his account of the ministry of Jesus with the calling of the disciples by the Sea of Galilee. But he stresses two things about Jesus. First, he came preaching the gospel of God. His method was preaching. I do not think preaching will ever be superseded by anything else. For preaching, in its essence, is the revealing of reality. It is letting people see what is actually here in life around us, the real truth about life. True preaching

I Cor. 1:21

is always that. In the words of Paul, ". . . by the open state-ment of the truth we would commend ourselves to every man's conscience in the sight of God" (2 Cor. 4:2). That is true preaching. And that is what Jesus came to do. He came to open the eyes of people to what was really happening in their lives.

Related to Reality

Second, his message was, "The kingdom of God is at hand; the time has come, the kingdom is at hand." What did he mean by "the kingdom of God"? Well, he meant all these things we have been talking about. The fact is that we are surrounded by an invisible spiritual kingdom with great forces, both of evil and of good, playing upon us. In that kingdom, Jesus is Lord; Jesus reigns supreme. And that kingdom governs all the events of history—all the events of our daily lives and circumstances. So that when we are related to the kingdom of God, we are related to the ultimate force which governs every-thing we are and have, and thus we are related to reality.

Jesus came with the good news that all the power of God is now available to break the helpless deadlock into which man has fallen Scripture tells us that man in his natural condition is helpless. No matter how much we like to think we are able to do something to correct our condition, we would be abso-lutely helpless and hopeless without the aid of God. In fact, human life would be impossible. Without God's mercy, with-out his restraining hand on forces that affect us, we could not even sit in the same room together—we would be at one another's throats, gouging out each other's eyes, hateful, and hating one another—animals, destroying ourselves.

But it is the mercy of God which keeps us from that. The good news is that a breakthrough has occurred. God's power has broken through. Jesus came to announce that the King is at hand, the One who can master a life, put it in order, bring peace and harmony into it, and supply a power which will produce a character no one else can rival. That is the kingdom of God. It is not meat and drink, says Paul, but righteousness and joy and peace in the Holy Spirit. The kingdom is at hand. And the place to gain it is the place of repentance, acknowledgment of need. To anyone and everyone who wants it, God's help is available, when you are willing to acknowledge that you cannot get along without it. That is why Jesus said, "Blessed are the poor in spirit, for theirs is the kingdom of heaven."

3

A Day in the Life of Jesus

It is a popular literary style today to trace through the events of one day in the life of a person. Alexander Solzhenitsyn has given us a remarkable book in *One Day in the Life of Ivan Denisovich*. Perhaps you have read some of Jim Bishop's books, like *The Day Kennedy Died* or *The Day Lincoln Died*. There is something similar in the Gospel of Mark, as Mark traces for us *A Day in the Life of Jesus*. It begins in the bright sunshine of a Galilean morning when Jesus walks out alongside the lake, moves into a mid-morning visit to a synagogue in Capernaum (for this was a sabbath day), takes in an afternoon visit some hours later at the home of Peter and Andrew, and traces the events of a busy evening in that city as thousands gathered to be ministered to by Jesus. The account concludes with a solitary prayer-vigil in the hills during the lonely hours of the early morning. Thus a full twenty-four hours is given to us in this account—put together from the brief memories Mark had of Jesus and the stories Peter had told him.

One theme is apparent as you read through the stories of the incidents in this day: the *authority* of Jesus, which Mark sees as stemming from the servant-character of Jesus. Although Mark would not understand at first how authority could come from being a servant, the theme that flows through all these accounts is a radical principle which is apparent in the Scriptures: To one who voluntarily serves, God gives the power also to rule.

Claim to Competence

There are six marks of the authority of Jesus recorded in this one day. The first is given to us in verses 16 through 20:

> And passing along by the Sea of Galilee, he saw Simon and Andrew the brother of Simon casting a net in the sea; for they were fishermen. And Jesus said to them, "Follow me and I will make you become fishers of men." And immediately they left their nets and followed him. And going on a little farther, he saw James the son of Zebedee and John his brother, who were in their boat mending the nets. And immediately he called them; and they left their father Zebedee in the boat with the hired servants, and followed him (Mk. 1:16–20).

It would be a great mistake to think that this is the first time Jesus ever saw these men. They were disciples of John the Baptist. Jesus had met them earlier down in Judea, and they had even followed him for a time as his disciples. So this is not their first encounter. But it *is* the story of their official call to a continual discipleship. The remarkable thing about this, the thing that impressed Mark, was Jesus' claim to *competence* in their lives. He said to them, "Follow *me* and *I* will make you become fishers of men." He assumes the entire responsibility for this.

These men were fishers of fish. They were simple Galilean fishermen, rough, somewhat ignorant, untutored, unlearned, elementary men, governed by Jewish passions and prejudices, narrow in their outlook. Before they could become fishers of men, they would have to become universal in their view. They would have to learn how to walk in a way that relied upon the power of the Spirit of God. And Jesus assumes the responsibility to do this. That is encouraging to me! Because whenever he calls you and me to any task, the Lord himself assumes the responsibility to fit us for it—if we follow him, if we yield to him.

In his book, *What Should This Man Do?*, Watchman Nee makes the very captivating suggestion that not only does Jesus undertake to equip these men fully for the task to which he calls them, but also he plans to do it in a way which retains the personality of each. This is suggested in what Mark records that these men were doing at the moment Jesus called them. Peter and Andrew were casting their nets into the sea, throwing circular nets out on each side of the boat in order to catch the fish. This suggests that they were to become evangelists. That would be their process of reaching out, casting out to those around. As the account goes on, we will see how Andrew becomes the disciple who leads people to Jesus, even as he has brought his brother Peter to Christ. Peter becomes the great evangelist when, on the day of Pentecost, he preaches the gospel to three thousand people.

But James and John were doing something else—they were mending their nets. The Greek word for "mending" is the same word which appears in Ephesians 4, where Paul says of pastor/teachers that they are to "equip" (or mend) the saints to do the work of the ministry. Just as James and John were equipping their nets—getting them ready—when Jesus called them, so this would be the work they would be doing as fishers of men. They would do it as teachers, equipping the saints. Again, this is what you see in the lives of these men throughout Scriptures.

This is a beautiful thought because it indicates that when our Lord calls us he not only equips us, taking full responsibility to teach us everything we need to learn in order to fulfill that calling, but he does it in such a way as to retain those nuances of personality that mark us as *us*.

When I was visiting Wheaton College one time, a young

student came up to me at the close of a chapel service and, with a very earnest look on his face, said, "Look, all week long you've been talking to us about Christ's working through us, saying that he will do the work. I have a question: How can Jesus work through us without destroying our personality?" I cast about for an answer, and all of a sudden an illustration came flashing into my mind: "When you prepare breakfast, if you plug an electric toaster and an electric mixer into the same outlet, would they both do the same thing?" He said, "I see what you mean." Of course they would not. They both use the same power, but they do not do the same thing. So it is with Jesus. He is the power in the Christian life, the One who is able to live in us and manifest himself through us—whatever the demand of life may be—but the result always retains something of our individuality. The glory of the call of Christianity is that we are all empowered by the same mighty One but that we lose nothing of the distinct flavor of our particular personality.

So Mark is impressed with this amazing competence of Jesus, for men simply do not act this way. Sign up for a course in personality development or management skills and invariably you are subjected to a standardizing process which tries to force everybody into the same mold. Unfortunately, we do this in Christian circles as well, so that we all come out of the sausage grinder as identical little sausages—chop it off anywhere and it is still boloney! But Jesus does not do that, and Mark marvels at the competence of this amazing man.

Comprehensive Scope

The second mark of authority he records in the following passage:

> And they went into Capernaum [Notice the word "they." Peter, Andrew, James, and John went with our Lord into Capernaum]; and immediately on the sabbath he entered the synagogue and taught. And they were astonished at his teaching, for he taught

them as one who had authority, and not as the scribes (Mk. 1:21–22).

Here Mark is amazed at the *comprehension* of Jesus, the vast scope of his knowledge, his insight into humanity and into life. He was particularly impressed with the authority with which he spoke. All who were present were astonished at his authority. He did not teach like the scribes they were accustomed to hearing: "Now, Hillel says this, and Gamaliel adds this, while other authorities contend . . ." Jesus made no reference to any authority other than himself. Yet his words were so insightful, so true to the experience and inner convictions of the men and women there that they nodded their heads, "Of course!" and knew what he said was true. J. B. Phillips entitled a book, *The Ring of Truth.* That is an apt description of how Jesus taught. His words had that ring of truth, acknowledged by all who heard him speak. It was self-authenticating truth, corresponding to an inner conviction in each person who heard him, so that they knew that he knew the secrets of life.

This is important, because it means that we ought to measure every teaching by what Jesus has said about the subject. I was at Wheaton College several years ago when the campuses of this nation were torn with riot and dissension, and even Christian colleges were not spared. I was invited to teach a class on current events, and we discussed various problems like capital punishment and, of course, the Vietnam War. I was greatly dismayed as I listened to these students because they constantly referred everything to secular authority. Finally, I stopped the class and said to them, "Look, this is a Christian college. Yet no one in this class has made any reference at all to what God has to say about these matters. But his, ultimately, is the only viewpoint that counts. And it is in what he says that the truth lies." Truth is what you find in the teachings of Jesus. We are to correct our psychology and our philosophy by the truth he sets forth.

I want to share with you a quotation I ran across some time
ago, from an outstanding American psychiatrist named J. T.
Fisher:

> If you were to take the sum total of all authoritative articles
> ever written by the most qualified of psychologists and psy-
> chiatrists on the subject of mental hygiene, if you were to
> combine them and refine them and cleave out the excess verbi-
> age, if you were to take the whole of the meat and none of the
> parsley, and if you were to have these unadulterated bits of pure
> scientific knowledge concisely expressed by the most capable of
> living poets, you would have an awkward and an incomplete
> summary of the Sermon on the Mount. And it would suffer im-
> measurably through comparison. For nearly two thousand years
> the Christian world has been holding in its hands the complete
> answer to its restless and fruitless yearning. Here rests the blue-
> print for successful human life, with optimum mental health
> and contentment.*

That is why, there in the synagogue at Capernaum, they
were astonished at the teaching of Jesus. And as I read through
the Scriptures and see the things that Jesus said, I am absolutely
dumbfounded at the amazing wisdom and insight into life that
he represents and at how he reveals how far afield secular thinking often is—how wrong it is when everybody around is prais-
ing it and saying it is right. That is why we need the insights
of this amazing man, as we study our lives, and human life in
general.

The Command of Truth

The next mark of the authority of Jesus is found in a very
remarkable response to the teaching of Jesus that sabbath
morning, verses 23 through 28:

---

* J. T. Fisher and L. S. Hawley, *A Few Buttons Missing* (Philadelphia: J. P.
Lippincott Company), p. 273.

And immediately there was in their synagogue a man with an unclean spirit; and he cried out, "What have you to do with us, Jesus of Nazareth? Have you come to destroy us? I know who you are, the Holy One of God." But Jesus rebuked him, saying, "Be silent, and come out of him!" And the unclean spirit, convulsing him and crying with a loud voice, came out of him. And they were all amazed, so that they questioned among themselves, saying, "What is this? A new teaching! With authority he commands even the unclean spirits, and they obey him." And at once his fame spread everywhere throughout all the surrounding region of Galilee (Mk. 1:23–28).

Mark sums it all up for us in the response of these people in the synagogue. They were astonished, amazed, and said, "With authority he commands even the unclean spirits, and they obey him." This represents the *command* of Jesus. There is no doubt that the unclean spirit in this man was reacting to the teaching of Jesus. He could not stand it! The insight our Lord gave on that morning was so piercing, so revealing of error and the foggy thinking of men, that the demon was tortured with truth, and he broke out in this angry interruption: "What have you to do with us, Jesus of Nazareth? I know who you are, the Holy One of God!" And Jesus rebuked him, commanded him to be silent.

Some years ago, the film, *The Exorcist,* so caught the popular imagination that people flocked in droves to see it. I did not see it myself, but I read several reviews of it made from various points of view. It is the story of a girl possessed by an evil spirit, a demon. She is supposedly set free of it by two men who intercede on her behalf. But from what I have heard and read of the film, I do not think it is quite what it seems to be. The girl may be freed temporarily from the evil spirit, but it is not a story of triumph over evil. It is the demon who triumphs, for he destroys the two men in the process. It is an evil and frightening film.

But you do not see anything of that here in this account.

When this demon is confronted with Jesus, he is forced to leave the person he was inhabiting. The word of Jesus is victorious right from the start. The spirit is reluctant to go, as is obvious from the way he convulses this person and cries out with a loud voice. But he *must* leave—that is the point. He is overwhelmed by a superior power. And through all the centuries since, the only name demons have ever feared is the name of Jesus. It is Jesus who sets men free and delivers the oppressed. It is well to remember, as we are experiencing in our own day a tremendous invasion of demonic forces, that no religious mumbo-jumbo or church ritual is going to set people free. It is Jesus whom demons fear—the authority of Jesus to command the unclean spirits to obey.

This particular obedience was so remarkable that Mark records, "And at once his fame spread everywhere throughout all the surrounding region of Galilee." When Mark says "at once," he does not mean in a few days or a few weeks; he means in a few hours. This was such a remarkable situation that within hours the word had spread like a flame all through the area. By evening, they were bringing the sick and demon-possessed into the city to be healed by Jesus, as we will see in a few moments. The word had gone out like wildfire that here was one who could command the spirits of darkness, and they would obey.

Jesus Took the Initiative

Next we have the account of a simple event in the home of Simon and Andrew, verses 29 through 31:

And immediately he left the synagogue, and entered the house of Simon and Andrew, with James and John. Now Simon's mother-in-law lay sick with a fever, and immediately they told him of her. And he came and took her by the hand and lifted her up, and the fever left her; and she served them (Mk. 1:29-31).

This is early afternoon by now, and Mark's emphasis is on the *compassion* that moved Jesus. If you read this account rather superficially, it sounds like a case of labor shortage. Simon and Andrew had invited Jesus and James and John home with them, only to find that the mother-in-law who perhaps usually did the serving was sick. So they apologized to Jesus, "told him of her." The English translation seems to suggest that they even asked him to heal her. But the Greek makes clear that this was not the case; it was Jesus' idea to heal her. When he heard about the sickness, he took the initiative, approached her, laid his hand upon her, and the fever left her. And it was out of a grateful heart that this restored woman ministered to the needs of these people that afternoon.

Now, it was not a necessary miracle; she was not particularly sick. The fever doubtless would have run its course, and she would have recovered in a few days. But it speaks of the compassion of the heart of Jesus that he responded to the suffering of this dear woman, light though it was, and touched her, delivered her, restored her to service that afternoon. Mark records for us that this is a compassionate Christ who ministers with such authority and power.

Then we have the evening account, verses 32 through 34:

That evening, at sundown, they brought to him all who were sick or possessed with demons. And the whole city was gathered together about the door. And he healed many who were sick with various diseases, and cast out many demons; and he would not permit the demons to speak, because they knew him (Mk. 1:32–34).

At sundown the sabbath ended, and they began to bring from the surrounding region all these sick and demon-possessed people for Jesus to heal. Mark tells us "the whole city was gathered together about the door." If you visit Capernaum today you will find it a very small town, perhaps a half dozen

houses. The ruins of a synagogue are there. Some have felt it
was the very synagogue in which Jesus taught. However, the
majority of scholarly opinion is that it dates from the second
century, although it was probably built on the site of the
synagogue described in this account. But at that time Capernaum was the most flourishing city on the lake, the largest city
of all. It was where Jesus made his home.

Vocal Quarantine

So people brought him their sick and diseased and demoniacs
to be healed. What a busy, full evening he spent there in
Capernaum! Mark records for us the amazing *control* Jesus
exercised over these demons. He laid a vocal quarantine upon
them. He would not permit them to speak because they knew
him. This is very significant, for it is the first indication of the
desire Jesus frequently manifested to de-emphasize the spectacular, to keep it under control, to play down deliverance
from demons and physical healing. On a number of occasions
Jesus said to those he healed, "Go and tell no man." That is,
"Don't tell anyone about this. Just accept your healing. But
don't spread the word around." Yet invariably they disobeyed
him, and soon it was recorded of him that he could no longer
come and minister in the city because of the crowds that followed him. It is evident that Jesus did not want those crowds
—not on those terms.

What a contrast this is with some people today. There are
healers who go about advertising their healing campaigns and
try to bring out the crowds on that basis, emphasizing the
spectacular in what they do. But you see nothing of this in the
Bible. Even with the apostles, the physical healings that went on
in their ministries were played down, just as with Jesus. They
never advertised them. There is no record in Scripture of people
giving public testimonials in order to increase the crowds, or of
being "zapped by the power of God," or any of the theatrics
you see so much of today. These are totally unbiblical.

Now, God does heal—and thank God for physical healings. But they are only temporary blessings at best. What Jesus continually emphasizes is the healing of the spirit of man— the healing of bitterness and hostility and lust and anger, of worry and anxiety and a critical spirit. This is what he is after —deliverance from these ugly and evil things, because this is of eternal value. The healing of the spirit is a permanent thing. So Jesus turns his back on popular acclaim, tries to suppress it and keep it under control, in order that he might be free for the ministry of greater importance.

Mark gives us the final account, the sixth picture, in verses 35 through 39:

And in the morning, a great while before day, he rose and went out to a lonely place, and there he prayed. And Simon and those who were with him followed him, and they found him and said to him, "Every one is searching for you." And he said to them, "Let us go on to the next towns, that I may preach there also; for that is why I came out." And he went throughout all Galilee, preaching in their synagogues and casting out demons (Mk. 1:35–39).

After this full day—and what a full day it was, what a heavy ministry our Lord had with all the healing he did in the evening!—Mark records that early in the morning, before it was daylight, Jesus went out on the mountainside and there, alone by himself, he prayed. But even there he was not safe. His disciples interrupted this *communion,* telling him that everyone was looking for him. And Jesus reveals the heart and substance of his prayer in what he says in reply: "Let us go on to the next towns, that I may preach there also; for that is why I came out." This is what he was praying about—that God would lead him, doors would be opened, and hearts prepared in the cities to which he would go next.

Why did Jesus seek the Father's face like this in these hours of pressure? The only answer we can come to is that he wants to make clear that the authority he had was not coming from him. This is what our Lord is trying to get across to us so continually in the Scriptures—that it was not his authority by which he acted; he had to receive it from the Father.

I do not know any more confusing doctrine in Christendom today—one which has robbed the Scriptures of their authority and power in the minds and hearts of countless people—than the idea that Jesus acted by virtue of the fact that he was the Son of God, that the authority and power he demonstrated were due to his own deity. Yet he himself takes great pains to tell us this is not the case. "The Son by himself can do nothing." Why do we ignore his explanation and insist that it is he, acting as the Son of God? He tells us that "it is not I; the Father who dwells in me, he does the works." And all the power that Jesus manifested had to come to him constantly from the One who dwelt within him.

Power to the Obedient

The reason Jesus stresses this is that this is what he wants us to learn. We are to operate on the same basis. Response to the normal, ordinary demands of life and power to cope with them must come from our reliance upon him at work within us. This is the secret—all power to live the Christian life comes not from us, doing our dead-level best to serve God, but from him, and is granted to us moment by moment as the demand is made upon us. Power is given to those who follow, who obey. The Father is at work in the Son: the Son is at work in us. As we learn this, then we are given power to meet the demands and needs which are waiting for us in the ministry yet to come.

This is why Jesus was up on the hillside praying—that there might be such a keenness of relationship with the Father that there would be no hindrance to the flow of the Spirit of God through him as he went out to these other cities. What a difference it makes when we begin to understand this principle!

This is what I labored to teach recently at a college campus. Many of the students caught on and came to us with exciting stories of what God had already done through them that very week, as they began to trust the power of God to work. One student said that he had gone home one evening thinking on the words, "Everything coming from God; nothing coming from me." As he tried to involve himself in his studies, his mind kept going out to his dad, who was not a Christian. So he phoned him and said, "Dad, the Billy Graham film, *Time to Run,* is in town; would you go with me tonight?" His father demurred, said he was tired. But the boy pressed him to go. His dad said, "All right, son, I haven't done anything with you for a long time. I'll go with you." They went, and he received the Lord that night. That boy was so excited to see God at work in him!

When I was in Mexico, I spent an evening with Miss Eunice Pike, the sister of Dr. Kenneth Pike—both of them noted and capable linguists. Miss Pike was telling me about the early days of Wycliffe Bible Translators in Mexico. Cameron Townsend, the founder, had gone to Mexico to try to get permission from the Mexican government to translate the Scriptures into the languages of the Indian tribes. The government was adamant that this should not take place. The official to whom he had to appeal said to him, "As long as I am in this office, you will never be given permission. We don't want the Bible in the Indian languages—it will only upset them." Townsend did everything he knew, went to every official he could find, had all his Christian friends praying that God would open this door. But it seemingly remained totally closed.

The Task at Hand

Finally he decided that he would give up pressing the issue, and he and his wife would go and live in a little, obscure Indian village, learn the language, minister to the people as best they could, and wait for God to move. They lived in a tiny trailer in this village. It was not very long before he noticed that the fountain in the center of the plaza produced beautiful, clear spring water, but it ran off down the hill and was wasted. He suggested that the Indians plant something in an area to which the water could easily be diverted, and thus make use of it. Soon they were growing twice as much food as before, and their economy blossomed as a result. The Indians were grateful. Townsend wrote this up in a little article and sent it to a Mexican paper he thought might be interested.

That article found its way into the hands of the President of Mexico, Lázaro Cárdenas. He said, "What is this? A gringo, an American coming here to live in an Indian village, where we can't even get our own people to live, and helping them this way? I must meet this man!" He ordered his limousine and his attendants, and they drove to that little Indian village. They parked at the plaza, and it happened that Townsend was there and saw the car. In response to his query, he was told it was the President of Mexico.

Cameron Townsend is not one to miss an opportunity. He went up to the car and introduced himself and, to his amazement, heard the President say, "You're the man I've come here to see!" He invited him to come to Mexico City and tell more about his work, and when he heard what it was, he said, "Of course! You can come to Mexico to translate the Scriptures into the Indian languages." That began a friendship which continued throughout the lifetime of President Cárdenas, who died just a few years ago. His power and authority were used of God all those years to open doors to Wycliffe translators throughout that country.

Only God can do things like that—bring the President down to see the peon! And that is what the church is missing in these days. We have everything so arranged and planned and strategized and overorganized that there is hardly any room for God to operate at all. But this is what Jesus knew—how God would work in his unique and wonderful way and open doors that nobody could anticipate, if he were the instrument ready and prepared to respond to that kind of power within.

How far removed that is from the way we all too often live today. God grant that as we study together, we will learn the great lessons Mark seeks to lay upon our hearts—that we are to live as Jesus lived, exactly as he lived, by the same power and force, and know that it is he working in us who does the work.

4

The Healer of Hurts

Mark is easy to follow because he gives us certain geographical clues which mark the divisions of this Gospel. He often ends a section with a summary statement like the one in verse 39: "And he [Jesus] went throughout all Galilee, preaching in their synagogues and casting out demons." The theme of that section, as we saw, is the authority of the servant—the authority which Jesus exercised. He commanded the disciples to follow him, and they came. He commanded the evil spirits, and they obeyed him. He commanded the fever to depart, and it left.

The next natural division encompasses chapter 1, verse 40, through chapter 3, verse 6. The theme of this division is the knowledge of humanity which Jesus displayed, his perceptive understanding of who we are and why we act the way we do. John the disciple precisely expresses this in the second chapter of his Gospel when he says,

Now when he was in Jerusalem at the Passover feast, many believed in his name when they saw the signs which he did; but Jesus did not trust himself to them, because he knew all men and needed no one to bear witness of man; for he himself knew what was in man (John 2:23–25).

That is a tremendously significant statement. It says that Jesus knew every individual who came to him. That is why he could say to Nathanael, "Before Philip called you, when you were under the fig tree, I saw you." That is why he could tell Nicodemus that he needed to be born again, and why he could say to the woman at the well, "You have had five husbands, and he whom you now have is not your husband . . ." He knew them because he knew what was *in man,* i.e., he understood humanity, how God made us, who we are. That is the theme Mark develops in this next section.

The first division includes two incidents in the life of Jesus: the healing of a leper, and the healing of a paralytic. These are tied together by the way they reveal truth about our basic humanity and about Jesus' perfect knowledge of this human nature. Let us look at this healing of the leper, which Matthew tells us took place immediately after the delivery of the Sermon on the Mount. As Jesus was coming down the mountain, this leper met him. Mark tells of the incident in this way:

> And a leper came to him beseeching him, and kneeling said to him, "If you will, you can make me clean." Moved with pity, he stretched out his hand and touched him, and said to him, "I will; be clean." And immediately the leprosy left him, and he was made clean (Mk. 1:40–42).

Mark highlights two impressive things about this miracle for us. First, the appeal of this leper to the will of Jesus. This **is** unique among the miracles. Second, the compassionate **response** with which Jesus answers this beseeching appeal.

No Claim to Healing

It is very significant that this leper said, *"If you will,* you can make me clean." Years ago a young man in our congregation came up to me. He had become very interested in the healing power of God and was involved in a movement which was teaching that healing is provided by God for every physical ailment we believers have, that it is wrong not to be well, and that we do not have to ask God whether he wants to heal us or not. This young man told me it is a lack of faith to pray, "If it be your will, heal me." He said we should claim our healing, and was very definite about it. I remember pointing out this incident to him—that the leper came to Jesus and said, "If you will, you can make me clean." And Jesus did not rebuke him or tell him he had approached him in the wrong way, or that he ought to claim his healing. In fact, you never find this idea in Scripture.

I think this indicates something of an awareness on the leper's part of a divine purpose there may have been in his affliction. It may perhaps be difficult for some of us to handle the concept, but the Scriptures are very clear that sometimes God wills us to be sick. Not that this is the expression of his ultimate desire for men, but that, given the circumstances in which we now live and the fallen nature of humanity, there are times when God wills for his children to pass through physical affliction. You see numerous examples of this in the Scriptures. Paul came before the Lord and asked three times for the removal of a physical "thorn in the flesh." Finally the answer came, "My grace is sufficient for you." Paul understood that God wanted him to put up with it and learn how to handle it by the grace of God. So it is clear that it is not the teaching of Scripture that everybody must be healed.

This leper is a case in point. Evidently he sensed some purpose in this, and when he said, "If you will, you can make me clean," he did not mean by that, "If you're in a good mood at present . . ." He meant, rather, "If it is not out of line with the purpose of God, if it is not violating some cosmic program God is working out, then you can make me clean." The action of Jesus is very positive: "Moved with pity, he stretched out

his hand and touched him, and said to him, 'I will; be clean.' "
That "I will" is like a green light from God. It says the time
has come for the healing to occur. Whatever purpose the
leprosy may have served, it has been accomplished and the time
has come to set it aside. "I will; be thou clean."

Mark says the immediate motive which moved Jesus was
pity, compassion. "Moved with pity, he stretched out his hand
and touched him." I love that "touch," which only Mark adds
here. He records that the response of Jesus' heart was to touch
him. Now, he was not drawn to him naturally. This was doubtless a very repulsive-looking man. Luke records, "he was full
of leprosy." William Barclay describes what a leper looks like:

> The whole appearance of the face is changed, till the man loses
> his human appearance and looks, as the ancients said, "like a
> lion or a satyr." The nodules grow larger and larger. They ulcer-
> ate. From them there comes a foul discharge. The eyebrows
> fall out, the eyes become staring. The voice becomes hoarse, and
> the breath wheezes because of the ulceration of the vocal cords.
> The hands and the feet always ulcerate. Slowly the sufferer be-
> comes a mass of ulcerated growths. The average course of the
> disease is nine years, and it ends in mental decay, coma, and
> ultimately death. The sufferer becomes utterly repulsive—both
> to himself and to others.*

Of course, worst of all is the sense of worthlessness and despair
this condition creates, which separates the sufferer from all
contact with humanity. It was this kind of man who came up
to Jesus and, breaking the law, dared to kneel before him and
beseech him, "Lord, if you will, you can make me clean." The
heart of Jesus was moved. He reached out and lovingly touched
him, and at that touch the leprosy vanished and the leper's
flesh was strong and clean once again. This is a beautiful
incident, illustrating the power of Jesus.

---

* William Barclay, *The Gospel of Mark* (Philadelphia: Westminster Press).

A Proof to Priests

But Mark immediately moves on to reveal to us the purpose which God intended for this incident, and which our Lord saw in it:

> And he sternly charged him, and sent him away at once, and said to him, "See that you say nothing to any one; but go, show yourself to the priest, and offer for your cleansing what Moses commanded, for a proof to the people" (Mk. 1:43–44).

Unfortunately, the Revised Standard Version confuses things a bit by substituting the words "to the people" for what the Greek really says. If you refer to the footnote, you will see that the Greek text is: "Go, show yourself to the priest, and offer for your cleansing what Moses commanded, for a proof *to them,*" i.e., the priests. This indicates what Jesus saw as the reason for this occurrence and the purpose he intended to accomplish. It was to be a witness to the priests, for they would be astonished when this man appeared to them and asked for the sacrifices Moses had commanded in the Book of Leviticus. You can understand how puzzled they were when this man came, wondering what to do, going to their libraries and getting down their books from the shelves, thumbing through them and saying to one another, "What will we do? There's never been anything like this since the days of Elisha! That's the last record of anyone being cleansed from leprosy. And even then it wasn't an Israelite, but a gentile, Naaman, commander of the Syrian armies." They would not know what to do.

Our Lord intended, clearly, that this would be for them a sign of the Messiah. Everyone in Israel, and especially the priests, knew that leprosy was a symbol of the evil and sin of man and that God used it as judgment, at times, in order to bring out in vivid, visible form what evil and sin are like in us. Now here was One who had power to cleanse the leper. Isaiah had predicted that when Messiah came, he would do certain physical miracles. The eyes of the blind would be opened, the lame would leap like the hart, the tongue of the dumb would sing, and lepers would be cleansed and healed. Now here is one of the signs of the Messiah which our Lord intended the priests should see as a witness to them of who he was.

Better Than Praise

But all of this was lost by the disobedience of this leper. Mark records it in verse 45:

> But he went out and began to talk freely about it, and to spread the news, so that Jesus could no longer openly enter a town, but was out in the country; and people came to him from every quarter (Mk. 1:45).

This leper proved to be a blabbermouth. He could not keep quiet, even though Jesus had *strictly charged* him, i.e., made clear to him that it was an important matter that he not tell anyone but the priests, that his witness be to the official representatives of the nation as a sign to them that Messiah was at hand. But all this was lost because the man succumbed to the inner desire of his heart to tell everyone what had happened. Now, it is understandable that he would feel this way. He had been cleansed from this loathsome, foul disease, and he longed to tell of it. I do not think our Lord ever intended that he should not tell of it, but only *after* he had borne witness to the priests. But this man could not wait, and in his eagerness he began to blaze the story abroad. I am sure he sang the praises of Jesus in doing so, but, nevertheless, this account is a careful testimony to us that obedience is better than praise.

We do this kind of thing very frequently. We do not need to point our finger at this man. I am amazed at how easily we set aside the Scriptures and disobey what God has said. We come up with some substitute—and praise God for it—when in reality it is disobedience. I have seen expensive, ornate buildings with bronze plates which say, "Erected to the glory of God," when God does not care for buildings at all. He cares for people. He never told us to put up any building for his glory. It is what happens in the lives of his people that glorifies God, not buildings erected to his name. So this man stands as a testimony to us of the need to obey what our Lord says, taking him simply at his word and doing what he says. He will be responsible for the results.

Because this leper did not do this, he hindered and limited the ministry of Jesus. Perhaps his ministry at Jerusalem would have been much more effective and powerful had this man done what Jesus asked him to do. But instead, although unwittingly and unintentionally, he violated the word of the Lord. As a result, a limitation was set upon Jesus. He could not come into the cities but had to stay in the countryside.

Mark moves right on to another healing, this time the healing of the paralytic in chapter 2. It falls into two major movements, the first centering around the faith of five men:

> And when he returned to Capernaum after some days, it was reported that he was at home. And many were gathered together, so that there was no longer room for them, not even about the door; and he was preaching the word to them. And they came, bringing to him a paralytic carried by four men. And when they could not get near him because of the crowd, they removed the roof above him; and when they had made an opening, they let down the pallet on which the paralytic lay. And when Jesus saw their faith, he said to the paralytic, "My son, your sins are forgiven" (Mk. 2:1–5).

The obvious thing Mark underscores for us here is the faith of these five men, the determination of their faith. They stand as an encouragement to us to exercise this kind of faith. It is important in understanding this story to see that this was not a healing service to which they came. Mark particularly tells us that Jesus was preaching the Word, and he was doing it in a house, not in the street. Relating this to the context, it is clear that he was avoiding the streets because they had been turned into a healing campaign. Everywhere he went people besieged him with requests for healing and the casting out of demons, so that he was unable to do what he had come to do primarily, which was to preach the Word.

So he had isolated himself in a house, and the room was jammed full of people. Even the doorway was blocked as people crowded around to hear the words of Jesus. But there were five men—the four who brought him and the man himself—who were determined to reach Jesus. Our Lord uses this incident to suggest to us that God is always open to the needs of people, regardless of whether they are physical, spiritual, or emotional. If their desire is strong enough, he will respond, despite the fact that it is not on the program. I love the times when the Spirit of God ignores the program! And this was not on the program for this meeting. But here were five men who longed to reach the Lord, were determined to do so, and their faith is a testimony and an encouragement to us.

This incident is a beautiful commentary on some words of Jesus that Matthew records. In Matthew 11:12 Jesus says, "From the days of John the Baptist until now the kingdom of heaven has suffered violence, and men of violence take it by force." Many have wondered what he meant by that. But God is simply saying, "Look, I'm ready to give to those who *really* want something." If you really want it, then God will give it, even though it is an interruption of the program he had in mind. So these men came—violently—ready to take what they knew God was offering at that moment and, in a sense, they took it by force.

Faith Dares

What is underscored here, of course, is the quality of faith. This is what faith is all about. There are three remarkable and beautiful aspects of it here. First, these men dared to do the difficult. That is where faith always manifests itself. It wasn't easy to bring this man to the Lord. They had to carry him, who knows how far, through the streets of the city—perhaps many blocks. And when they found the doorway blocked, they had to carry him up an outside stairway to the roof. We do not know how heavy he was, but it is not easy to carry a full-grown man up a flight of stairs. Yet these men managed this difficult task. They dared to do the difficult.

Then, notice that they dared to do the unorthodox. They were not limited by the fact that it was not at all customary to break up a roof. When they found that the door was blocked, they did not sit down, as we probably would have done, and appoint a committee to research the various ways to get to Jesus. No, they just did what was necessary and risked the disapproval not only of the owner of the house but also every person there by interrupting the meeting in order to get their friend to Jesus. The remarkable thing is that Jesus never rebuked them, never criticized their interruption. He never does. There is never an incident recorded in which Jesus got uptight or disturbed about an interruption by someone intent on receiving something from him and pressing through to him despite the disapproval of those around.

I love that quality in Christianity. I hope we never lose it—this ability to defy the status quo. Nothing is more deadly in a church than the attitude of "Come weal or woe; our status is quo," because the members are afraid to do anything which might be criticized. But these men dared to do the unorthodox.

Third, they dared to do the costly. Somebody had to pay for that roof. Imagine the face of the owner, sitting there at the feet of Jesus, when he hears this scratching on the roof. He looks up and, to his amazement, the tiles begin to move. Then daylight appears, and suddenly he has a large hole in his roof! I do not know what his thoughts were. He probably wondered if his Homeowner's Policy would cover it or not! Or maybe he was mentally adding up the bill to present to these men. But somebody had to pay that bill, somebody had to repair that roof, and surely it was one, if not all, of these men. They dared to do the costly. That is faith! They laid it on the line—at cost to themselves. What a witness this is to what it takes to bring people to Christ!

Mark has emphasized all this in order that we might move to the second part of the passage which gathers around the protest of the scribes. Here we learn the heart of this story. Jesus had said to the paralytic, "Your sins are forgiven."

> Now some of the scribes were sitting there, questioning in their hearts, "Why does this man speak thus? It is blasphemy! Who can forgive sins but God alone?" And immediately Jesus, perceiving in his spirit that they thus questioned within themselves, said to them, "Why do you question thus in your hearts? Which is easier, to say to the paralytic, 'Your sins are forgiven,' or to say 'Rise, take up your pallet and walk'? But that you may know that the Son of man has authority on earth to forgive sins"—he said to the paralytic—"I say to you, rise, take up your pallet and go home." And he rose, and immediately took up the pallet and went out before them all; so that they were all amazed and glorified God, saying, "We never saw anything like this!" (Mk. 2:6–12).

It is evident from the words of Jesus that this paralysis was caused by some moral difficulty. Our Lord's insight is accurate and keen. He understood instantly what was wrong with this man. Notice that he does not touch on the physical at first; he goes right to the heart of the problem: "Son, your sins are forgiven." In fact, Matthew tells us he said, "Son, be of good cheer; your sins are forgiven." This indicates that the paralysis was what doctors sometimes call "emotionally induced" illness. That is, something in this man's past or present, some attitude he harbored, some feeling he indulged, was causing the paralysis.

Doctors have said that 50 percent of all the illnesses they

treat are emotionally caused. Not that they are not genuine—
the people who have them really are ill—but they are caused
by some emotional problem. Many things can result in this type
of illness: A bitter spirit, a lack of forgiveness, harboring a
grudge against somebody—any of these will, over a long span
of years, turn the life sour and affect the body and mind to the
point where it loses its capacity to function. We know that
ulcers are emotionally induced, primarily. Somebody has said
that ulcers are caused not by what you eat but by what is eating
you! Guilt can affect us physically. Perhaps this man had done
injury to someone and bore a heavy burden of guilt, was unable to forgive himself, and looked back upon the past and
dwelt on it until it affected his body so it would not function.

Jesus, knowing that this man was paralyzed because of some
moral problem, immediately went to the heart of the problem.
He touched him and said, "Son, your sins are forgiven." If he
had simply healed the paralysis without having forgiven the
sin, there is no doubt that the paralysis would have returned
sooner or later. This is what accounts for many of the so-called
miracles of healing in the healing services we hear and read
about today. These involve emotionally induced problems—
physical, yes, but caused by some emotional problem. And the
momentary atmosphere of excitement and faith generated by
such a meeting is often enough to effect a temporary change.
People may be freed, for the moment, from their difficulty and
give witness to that effect. But medical investigators have
proven again and again that within a matter of days those same
illnesses return. (You do not hear so much of that—only of
the healings!) But our Lord went to the heart of the matter
and forgave this man's sins, so that the healing he received
would last and the paralysis never return.

Puzzled Scribes

This was a problem to the scribes sitting nearby. They were
puzzled, and our Lord understood that. Notice how Mark puts

this. These scribes were questioning *"in their hearts."* They did not say anything; they did not even talk among themselves. Jesus read their thoughts and their hearts. He knew in his spirit that they questioned within themselves. You can imagine the startled looks on their faces when our Lord turned to them and said, "Why are you fellows thinking that way? I know what you're thinking."

I know that some interpret this as evidence of what they call the omniscience of Jesus, and conclude that he was acting as God here. I do not think so. We must never forget that there was an occasion when he said specifically that he, as a man, did not know something. He did not know the hour of his return; only the Father knew that (Matt. 24:36). No, this is not omniscience; it is, rather, the manifestation of the spiritual gift of discernment in its fullest degree. You see Peter doing the same thing when Ananias and Sapphira came to him. He knew all about their fraud, even though no one had told him. When Paul was confronted on the island of Cyprus by a magician named Bar-Jesus, he knew what was going on in that man's life, knew his attitude of heart. This is the gift of discernment.

Our Lord knew what was going on in the minds of these scribes, and so he proposed a test to them: "Which is easier to say, 'Your sins are forgiven,' or 'Take up your bed and walk'?" Notice how he put that. He did not say, "Which is easier *to do?*" Because obviously it is much easier to heal a man physically than to forgive his sins. Only God can forgive sins; they are right about that. Only the offended can remit the offense, and only God has the right to forgive sins. It is much easier to heal a body—a physician can do that. But he said, "Which is easier *to say?*" Obviously, any charlatan, any religious racketeer, can say to a man, "Your sins are forgiven," and no one could prove whether it happened or not. So that is easier to say. Our Lord is saying to these men, "You question my ability to forgive sins. I'm going to demonstrate to you that I not only have the power to forgive sins, but I have the power to heal as well—which is easier to do but harder to say, because you can verify it." And turning to the paralyzed man, he said, "Rise, take up your bed and go home." And the man obeyed, instantly healed. He walked out of their midst. And all the people—except for the scribes—rejoiced and gave glory to God, saying, "We never saw anything like this!"

What amazed them? Not merely the healing. They had seen healing miracles before. What amazed them was Jesus' understanding of the problems of human nature. What amazed them was the fact that he understood so clearly that physical and emotional problems are often caused by spiritual disease and maladjustment, that the center of security and deliverance and liberty lies in what goes on between a man and God. This is what amazed them.

This is the lesson we find so difficult to learn. We are all seeking the secret of adequacy. How can you handle life? How can you be poised and confident and courageous? How can you be freed from inner tensions and turmoil and anxiety and insecurity? We struggle to try to do it on the level of our relationships with one another, trying to heal our relationship with a neighbor, or our wife, or children. And we ignore this great revelation to us. Our healing begins with our relationship to God. Only the man who has heard Jesus say, "Your sins are forgiven," is free from that tension within, thus enabling him to cope with life outside.

The amazing truth is that you will treat other people just as you think God treats you, and you cannot escape that. Not the way you *say* God treats you—using all the religious phrases and quoting all the nice biblical verses. God knows, and your heart knows, that it is not true, and it will all come out in the way you think God is toward you. If you see him as loving, understanding, forgiving, patient, then that is how you will treat others. There is no way around it. It all starts with the kind of relationship you have with him.

This is why Jesus went right to the heart of the problem and said, "Your sins are forgiven." Paul says in his letter to the Ephesians that you are chosen of God, and precious. Do you think of yourself that way? Every morning when you wake up, that is what you ought to say of yourself—chosen of God, precious to him. Because that will set your spirit free to be available to help somebody else with his problems, for all your inner tensions and turmoil are settled. That is liberty, that is freedom, that is where confidence is born—in faith that God himself lives in you and is ready to work through you, taking the ordinary things you do and imparting to them the touch of heaven, so that unusual, extraordinary results will accrue which perhaps you know nothing about.

This is how God intends us to live and is what this little incident sets forth. Our Lord understood the need of this man and instantly went to the heart of it. He said, "Son, the thing you need more than anything else is forgiveness of sins. Be of good cheer; your sins are forgiven." From then on it was the easiest thing; it took but the flick of his finger to dismiss the paralysis. That is what God can do in your life and mine.

5

The Scandal Maker

Many view Jesus in the way he is often pictured—as a very weak and mild man who sought always to live at peace with everyone and who avoided controversy whenever possible. But as you read the Gospel accounts, you see that from the very beginning he deliberately provoked certain groups. He never hesitated to flout the petty regulations of men, and he knowingly and deliberately offended people. In fact, he became too hot to handle, and the "establishment" of that day finally decided that the only way out was to get rid of him. We need this view of Jesus to balance the false impressions we often acquire. But we need to keep the entire picture in balance. He was no radical revolutionist, as we use the term today. He did challenge the status quo, but never in a violent or desperate way.

In the passage in Mark's Gospel we come to now, we have an account of the kind of controversy Jesus constantly raised. This controversy came out of his penetrating knowledge of human nature and his unceasing opposition to anything which threatened true humanity. Remember that the theme of this division of Mark is Jesus' knowledge of man. We have seen the clarity of that knowledge reflected in the healings of the leper and the paralytic. In the final section of this division Mark brings together four incidents which reveal the refusal of Jesus to be boxed in by purely human regulations and his deliberate provocation of controversy in order that the true nature of freedom might be made evident. The stage for the first of these incidents is set by the calling of Matthew to be a disciple:

> He [Jesus] went out again beside the sea; and all the crowd gathered about him, and he taught them. And as he passed on, he saw Levi the son of Alphaeus sitting at the tax office, and he said to him, "Follow me." And he rose and followed him (Mk. 2:13–14).

Levi was evidently Matthew's given name. It is likely that Jesus is the one who changed his name to Matthew, as he renamed several disciples. He said to Simon the son of Jonas, "You shall be called Peter," i.e., "rock." He nicknamed James and John, the sons of Zebedee, "sons of thunder." So it is very likely (although Scripture does not say so) that it was Jesus who changed Levi's name to Matthew, which means "gift of God." Perhaps that is how Jesus thought of him.

Levi lived and worked in Capernaum, where Jesus had made his home. He was a tax collector there and must have known of Jesus and heard him speak, even before this call. This was not his first encounter with Jesus. It is really remarkable that Jesus would call a man like this, for tax men were no more loved then than they are now. In fact, these tax collectors were very often hated. For the most part, they were trained extortioners, making their living by taxing the people beyond what the law demanded. They were paid no salary—only given the opportunity to fleece everyone they collected from. They did have to turn in a certain percentage to the government, according to law, but they kept the rest. They were usually rich

men, but were hated by all for their practices. But Jesus saw
something in Levi—knew his heart, knew there was something
in him which made him discontented with this kind of life.
He saw the hunger of his heart. Therefore he called him, and
said, "Follow me." He cared nothing at all that it would damage
his own reputation to allow such a man to be a disciple.

Collection of Rascals

The next scene probably occurred the following day, and it
is associated by Mark with the call of Matthew:

> And as he [Matthew] sat at table in his house, many tax col-
> lectors and sinners were sitting with Jesus and his disciples; for
> there were many who followed him. And the scribes of the
> Pharisees, when they saw that he was eating with sinners and
> tax collectors, said to his disciples, "Why does he eat with tax
> collectors and sinners?" And when Jesus heard it, he said to
> them, "Those who are well have no need of a physician, but
> those who are sick; I came not to call the righteous, but sinners"
> (Mk. 2:15–17).

This was evidently a farewell dinner that Matthew gave for
his friends, his tax-collecting buddies. He was saying farewell
to his work and friends and leaving to follow One who would
travel from place to place. It was also an opportunity to introduce them to his new-found Lord. It was, therefore, a normal,
natural occasion of festivity and joy as they gathered together
for this feast.

What a collection of rascals must have been there that day!
All the tax collectors of the city, all the sinners, all the despised
social outcasts were sitting there. As the scribes of the Pharisees
passed by, they saw that right in the midst of it all, among the
"beer bottles and the poker chips," sat Jesus. And they were
absolutely scandalized! It was obvious that he was the friend
of these men. He was not lecturing them. He was sitting among
them, and eating and drinking with them. The scribes were

simply appalled at this and called the disciples aside: "Why does he do things like that? Doesn't he know who these people are? Why does he allow himself to be seen in the company of such men?"

Jesus' answer is very revealing. He actually agrees with their remarks. He says, in effect, "You're right, these are sick, hurting, troubled men. Their style of life has damaged them deeply. They don't see life rightly; they are covering up many evils; they are false in many ways. You're right, these *are* sick men. But where else would a doctor be?" That is his argument: "I've come to heal men, and where they are hurting is where I'm needed."

In that marvelous way he has of putting things, he says something to them which directs their attention to the right focus but also turns their gaze back toward themselves. He says, "I came to call not the righteous, but sinners." That is, those who think they are righteous, as these Pharisees did, are actually more needy than those they regard as social outcasts. These Pharisees were actually more deeply disturbed than the tax collectors and sinners, but they did not know it. But Jesus was saying to them, "To those who think they're righteous, I have absolutely nothing to say. But to these who know they're sick, and are open for help, I am fully available as a minister to their souls."

The Terrible Illusion

Our Lord made several things emphatically clear by this reply. First, he indicated very strongly that when people think they have no need of help from God, they are in no position to be helped. There is nothing to say to them. We meet people today who are "self-sufficient," who think they do not need God at all. I have long ago learned that the best way to treat them is to smile and be friendly and let them go their way. Life itself will teach them they are wrong. Sooner or later the bottom will drop out, and all their dreams of self-reliance will collapse about their feet. Then is the time you can talk to them; then they will be listening.

This is why God often allows trouble into our lives. It makes us stop clinging to the terrible illusion that we are able to handle life by ourselves. That is the greatest delusion spread among men. As long as people think that, there is little you can do for them, and not much you can say. But our Lord always put his efforts where men and women were open to help, where they were hurting so much they knew they needed help. This past week I met a man and spent some time talking with him. He had been a self-sufficient, "self-made" man, a prominent lawyer. But now everything had collapsed. His wife was leaving him, his business had failed, and he had thought of suicide several times. For the first time he understood that he could not handle life, and he was wide open to listen to someone who would tell him of the Great Physician.

The second thing our Lord reveals is that people are more important than prejudice. Oh, that we would learn that! Prejudices are preconceived notions formed before we have sufficient knowledge, usually mistaken or distorted ideas we have grown up with. When prejudices are in opposition to the needs of men, they are to be swept aside without any hesitation. People are more important than prejudices, and Christians must learn that. The Christian church has been criticized and denounced and forsaken, and justifiably so, because of the prejudices it still manifests in terms of class, race, financial, and even sex distinctions. We Christians must learn to ignore all differences of class, social station, race, wealth, and sex and meet all alike according to their readiness of heart. Whenever you find someone hungry, hurting, and needing help—whether he is dressed in gabardine and works in a financial center, or is a savage in the jungle, or a workman in a shop, or a hippie living in the forest—that is the person who needs the Great Physician; that is the one to whom friendship should be extended.

We Christians must learn to treat people like this, regardless of what their outward appearance may be. We must learn to see the waiter and waitress, the newsvendor, the bellboy, the elevator operator, as people whose hearts may be in need. We need not be at all impressed with the topflight executive. He, too, is a man who may be hurting and needing help. That is the way Jesus approached people everywhere. He was looking for those who were ready to respond because of the hurt of their life. I love the words of C. T. Studd, the brilliant young Englishman, who gave away a fortune that he might go out to the forests of Africa. He put his philosophy this way:

> Some like to dwell
> Within the sound
> Of church and chapel bell.
> But I want to run a rescue shop
> Within a yard of Hell.

That was the philosophy of Jesus, too.

Flouting Tradition

The second incident deals with the power of tradition. Mark says, beginning in verse 18:

Now John's disciples and the Pharisees were fasting; and people came and said to him, "Why do John's disciples and the disciples of the Pharisees fast, but your disciples do not fast?" And Jesus said to them, "Can the wedding guests fast while the bridegroom is with them? As long as they have the bridegroom with them, they cannot fast. The days will come, when the bridegroom is taken away from them, and then they will fast in that day" (Mk. 2:18–20).

Once again we have a group of offended Pharisees. Evidently the day on which this incident occurred was a fast day. The law of Moses required only one day of the year to be a fast day—

the day known as Yom Kippur, or the Day of Atonement, which the Jews observe to this day. But the Pharisees, in order to show how zealous they were, had through the centuries designated more and more days as fast days, for they regarded fasting as the best way to get God's attention—and, incidentally, to call the attention of men to their piety. This is why the Pharisees put on sackcloth (burlap), rubbed ashes on their faces, and sucked in their cheeks so they would look gaunt—to call people's attention to how pious and righteous they were. And they hoped God would take notice, too.

This evidently was one of those customary fast days, and some people came to Jesus and said, "Why do John's disciples and the disciples of the Pharisees fast, but your disciples do not fast? Everybody else is keeping this fast," they said. "Why do you flout the traditions like this? Why do you deliberately ignore these customs? Why don't you make your disciples fast?" This type of question is often asked today: "Why don't you keep the regulations? Why don't you keep the rules? Why does your particular group feel it doesn't have to adhere to the same standards as everybody else?"

Our Lord's answer again is very suggestive. In effect, what he says is, "You've misunderstood entirely the nature of the occasion. You think it is a funeral, but it's not; it's a wedding. A bridegroom is here. And at a wedding nobody fasts. As long as the bridegroom is there, there will be festivity—rejoicing, laughter, and gladness. Now, there will come a day when the bridegroom will be gone, and then it is all right to fast. But when the bridegroom is present there is feasting, not fasting." Of course, there was a predictive element in his statement. He indicated there would come a day when he would leave these men, and then they would indeed fast and mourn. But as these words apply to us, that day never comes—or never need come. There are times of mourning in our life, times of sorrow. But in every such instance there is always the availability of Jesus Christ to step into the situation and turn it into a feast day.

A Different Kind of Worship

In these words our Lord is putting his finger upon the nature of the new relationship he had come to demonstrate and to bring to men—what it would be like and what it would mean in terms of activity and expression. All this time the Jews had worshiped in the temple—solemn, ceremonial, ritualistic services centering upon sacrifice and silence before the greatness of God. Now our Lord is teaching them that a new relationship has come in which there is a vitality and a warmth of intimacy with the bridegroom himself which can be expressed only in terms of joy and gladness and celebration.

This is what we Christians need to see again. Jesus is commenting here upon the drastic changes in the character of worship which occur when people discover the reality of relationship with Jesus Christ. Church services, for far too many centuries, have been borrowed from an Old Testament concept of worship and have presented a scene of solemnity and silence and ritual. This predominated in the Roman Catholic Church, and it has been carried over unthinkingly into Protestant churches as well, so that even today we suffer from the attitude that a church service ought to be a time of silence, when everyone sits in supposed awestricken solemnity before God. But this is not the picture Jesus came to give. "No," he says, "instead of the fast, it is a feast, instead of the sackcloth, there is a robe; and instead of solemnity, there ought to be joy."

One reason why so much of the church today is written off by people who have come to see what Christians are like is the morbidity and dullness of what we call worship. In many church services across this land today the diet is what can only be described as predictable pablum, dished-up Pollyanna, as dull and unexciting as can be! Many services are so totally predictable that, without being present, you can look at your watch and, at any given moment, say what is happening. The preaching which comes forth is so shallow and repetitive that people have turned off their ears and no longer listen. Why they subject themselves to coming at all, I do not understand. I honestly do not blame those who do not come. Church people complain that men are out playing golf and boating on Sunday morning. But until the church recovers the excitement and joy of a wedding feast and the people are gladsome of heart, they cannot be blamed for not coming. When the church does recover what Jesus has indicated here, then the meetings will be full again.

Our Lord highlights this difference with two very perceptive and vivid illustrations:

> "No one sews a piece of unshrunk cloth on an old garment; if he does, the patch tears away from it, the new from the old, and a worse tear is made. And no one puts new wine into old wineskins; if he does, the wine will burst the skins, and the wine is lost, and so are the skins; but new wine is for fresh skins" (Mk. 2:21-22).

No one could illustrate better than Jesus. How he would take these simple, commonplace things which were part of everyday life, and make them speak the truths he wanted to illustrate with freshness and clarity! He is talking about this new relationship when the bridegroom is in their midst and there is the joy and celebration of the feast. "When you have that kind of a relationship with me," he says, "then it is no longer the time to try to patch up the old with the new."

New Forms for New Life

What did he mean by that? Fresh relationships require new expressions! When you are going on in the old way—and everything has the tendency to get old after awhile—the quality of relationship is affected. The warmth and joy often depart. Then, when something brings a new awakening—a fresh sense of the presence of God—do not try to express it through the old forms. It will not work. The new is too power-ful and will destroy those old forms which try to contain it. You cannot do it that way.

We have an example of this today in the fresh awakening of the Spirit which has moved through this country since the late 1960s. In place after place, people are trying to put this back into the old, familiar forms of church service and are finding it will not work. It must be done in a new way. Instead of sitting there with folded hands, solemn and pious, even morbid, in the presence of God, showing no response at all, people are manifesting the joy they feel, as Christ has come as a living Person into their lives, by clapping their hands, putting their arms around others, and manifesting loving relationships in that way. To resist this is to fall into the error Jesus has so vividly delineated for us here—putting an unshrunk patch on an old garment. As the patch shrinks, it tears a hole larger than before.

The second illustration is similar—new wine cannot be put into old wineskins. They did not have bottles in those days, but used sewed up animal skins. The old ones became brittle, inflexible, and burst easily. New wine is strong and is still fermenting, giving off gases. If you put new wine into old wineskins, soon it will burst the old skins and everything will be lost. Jesus means by this that strong reactions (for wine is the symbol of joy) need fresh controls. Wineskins are made to hold wine, but they have to be flexible. They cannot be rigid and unbending and inflexible, but must be able to expand with the wine, expressing the joy they contain. Our Lord, in great wisdom, is showing us here what happens when a people or an individual returns to a vital relationship with Christ. They must find new ways to express it and not go back to the old ways. This is what the Spirit of God is showing us so vividly in these days.

The principle our Lord is illustrating here is that tradition must never be permitted to destroy relationships. That is what often happens. We have to fight tradition. Jesus fought it in his own day. It was the most pernicious and subtle foe he encountered. Everywhere he turned he found himself in face-to-face combat with the rigid traditions of the past—the dead hand of the past locking in the present. He was ever opposed to that. And so we must learn to become the foe of traditions which violate relationships.

The third incident touches on the problem of rules, beginning at verse 23:

> One sabbath he was going through the grainfields; and as they made their way his disciples began to pluck ears of grain. And the Pharisees said to him, "Look, why are they doing what is not lawful on the sabbath?" And he said to them, "Have you never read what David did, when he was in need and was hungry, he and those who were with him: how he entered the house of God, when Abiathar was high priest, and ate the bread of the Presence, which it is not lawful for any but the priests to eat, and also gave it to those who were with him?" And he said to them, "The sabbath was made for man, not man for the sabbath; so the Son of man is lord even of the sabbath" (Mk. 2:23–28).

Those were challenging words to these men. Once again, we have an incident that put him in direct confrontation, immediate controversy with these Pharisees. Now his disciples were doing what would have been perfectly proper on any weekday. They were not stealing from this farmer as they went through his grainfields, for the law said that as long as they did not put a sickle or a scythe to the grain, any passing travelers who were hungry could thresh out a few heads of grain in their hands and eat the wheat. The problem was that this was the sabbath, and by this time the sabbath had had a thousand and one restrictions built into it by the Pharisees.

The sabbath originally was given to restore man, to give him rest and recreation. Properly observed, it would be a joy. But the Pharisees had so ringed it about with their thousands of interpretations of what it meant to cease work that they had made it a terrible burden to bear. For instance, they held that it was perfectly all right to spit on a rock on the sabbath—that presented no problem. But if you spat on the ground, that made mud, mud was mortar; therefore you were working on the sabbath. So it was absolutely wrong to spit on the ground! That was the nature of the restrictions they devised. So it is not surprising that they considered it wrong to thresh a head of grain on the sabbath day, even though you were hungry, because that was working on the sabbath.

Rules to Be Broken

Jesus skewered them on their own sword: the Scriptures. They were supporting their regulations and defending their laws by the commandment, "Remember the sabbath day, to keep it holy. Six days you shall labor, and do all your work; but the seventh day is a sabbath to the Lord your God; in it you shall not do any work . . ." But Jesus said, "Wait a minute. Have you never read 1 Samuel 21? David and his men, fleeing for their lives, were hungry. There was no ordinary food available, so in desperation they entered the tabernacle, went into the holy place, took the showbread, which the law that God himself had given said was designated for the priests only, and ate it. Twelve loaves of bread, standing as a symbol for Israel, prepared fresh each week, were placed on the table in the tabernacle. After a week, the priests, and only the priests, could eat it. But David, because of the hunger of his men, dared to go in and take those loaves of bread and pass them out among them. And God did not do anything about it. Now what do you make of that?"

Well, they do not give any reply. So Jesus draws a conclusion: "The sabbath was made for man, not man for the sabbath. And the Son of man (the quintessential man) is lord even of the sabbath." By this he underscores the principle which must govern our lives as believers: human needs always take precedence over rules. Hunger is healthy and, therefore, holy. It is wrong to make rules which stop men from satisfying the basic need of their lives. This is why we must examine the systems of our day. It is easy to focus on a single act and say, "That breaks a rule." Yes, but why is it broken? That is what society and the church must ask. Did we force this individual, by means of the system in which he lives, to do something illegal in order to satisfy a basic need of his life? If so, then there is something wrong with the system. This is what Jesus was forcing them to examine. The sabbath was made to restore men, but when it became a burden and a hindrance, then it was wrong. Those man-made regulations needed to be broken, and our Lord broke them.

Some years ago we sent a team of men to minister at a midwestern college. We were holding meetings in a large room in the women's dormitory. There was a rule at that college that the girls had to be in their rooms at 10:30 P.M. The boys could stay out till 12:00, but the girls had to be in bed at 10:30. We were having a great meeting. God had broken through in a remarkable way. These kids had begun for the first time to relate to each other as people, and were going to one another, apologizing and being forgiven, standing weeping together with their arms around each other, praying for one another—it was a great movement of the Spirit.

Promptly at 10:30 the dorm mother appeared, looking like a thunderstorm. She said, "It is 10:30, and time for these girls to be in their rooms!" One of us said, "But God is working here, and we can't stop this meeting now." She said, "I'm the dorm mother here, and the rule requires that they be in bed at 10:30, and I'm going to see that it's observed!" One of us had the sense to say, "Well, we understand your problem. Could we go in and talk with you about it?" And so we sent one fellow in—who talked for two and one-half hours while the meeting went on!

But that is the way we tend to think: Bedtime must be observed, no matter what. Regulations of conduct in the home must always be observed, taking precedence over everything else. But Jesus says, "No, human need takes precedence over rules." Rules are orderly ways to meet needs. That is what they are for. And they are perfectly right in that way. But when a rule actually ends up opposing the meeting of the need, then the rule has to go. Our Lord is the first to make that clear.

The last incident deals with the danger of zealous pride:

> Again he entered the synagogue, and a man was there who had a withered hand. And they watched him, to see whether he would heal him on the sabbath, so that they might accuse him. And he said to the man who had the withered hand, "Come here." And he said to them, "Is it lawful on the sabbath to do good or to do harm, to save life or to kill?" But they were silent. And he looked around at them with anger, grieved at their hardness of heart, and said to the man, "Stretch out your hand." He stretched it out, and his hand was restored. The Pharisees went out, and immediately held counsel with the Herodians against him, how to destroy him (Mk. 3:1-6).

This is a crucial moment in the ministry of Jesus, marking the climax of a growing hostility which you can trace through the questions asked by these Pharisees. The first one is rather mild: "Why does he eat with tax collectors and sinners?" The second is a little more serious: "Why do John's disciples fast, and the disciples of the Pharisees fast, but your disciples do not fast?" The third is even more crucial: "Why are you doing what is not lawful on the sabbath?" The fourth brings before us the statement: "They watched him . . . so that they might accuse him." The hostility is sharpened, the synagogue door is closing to Jesus, and these men have now become his open and avowed enemies.

But they paid him a remarkable compliment. They came into that synagogue knowing that there was present a man with a withered hand. They knew without a doubt that Jesus would

not be up in the front talking to the priest; he would be concerned about that man with the withered hand. They knew
they could trap him that way.

Evil Exposed

Notice how Jesus handled this. He deliberately called the
man into the center, turned a spotlight on him and said, "I
don't want any of you to miss this. Come here." And the man
stood there in the midst of them. While he was standing there,
Jesus turned to the Pharisees and asked two very penetrating
questions. He said, in effect, "You're concerned about the sabbath, aren't you? Let me ask you: whose thoughts are nearer to
the purpose of the sabbath—yours or mine?" For he read their
thoughts. "I want to do good to this man, while you want to
harm me. I want to save this man and heal him; you're thinking
of killing me. Now, which is in line with the sabbath?" Mark
says they were silent. No wonder.

Then, angered at their hardness of heart, grieved by their
resistance, Jesus healed the man, thus underscoring for us that
an excess of zeal (which is what motivated these men in their
rules and regulations concerning the sabbath) is destructive and
was invalidating something perfectly good. There is nothing
wrong with the sabbath as God gave it to man. But these men
so heaped it with rules and regulations that they had destroyed
it. Their zeal to maintain it had ruined it. Jesus cut across all
that. Mark records that their immediate reaction was to be so
angry at the threat he represented to their favored position in
society that they immediately went out and joined their enemies,
the Herodians, in taking counsel how they might destroy him.
This is where Jesus always drove evil—right out into the open,
where it was visible to all.

We are confronted with many of these same situations, so
we need to ask ourselves why Jesus acted in this way. Why did
he deliberately provoke controversy and hostility? Our reason
is often that we have a certain cause we are trying to advance.

Most of the revolutionaries and politicians of today are trying to attack another group, because they are defending their own. They feel it is necessary to destroy the other group in order to uphold their own ideals. But our Lord did not do that. Even though he pointed out things which were wrong, he never was harsh in his words or his attitude towards men. He was grieved and hurt, but he was not harsh. Nor was he ever garish or outlandish. He never did things merely for the sake of being different. He did not try to call attention to himself by bizarre actions, by walking around with a cross on his back, or beating himself in public, or wearing strange clothes, or looking remarkably different from anybody else.

And yet, having said all that, neither was he ever fearful or compromising. The answer, of course, is the principle which governed his actions: he was simply true to truth, always. He reacted as God had made man to be, and disregarded anything which stood in the way. That is why he did these things. He refused to allow all the rules and petty traditions and regulations and prejudices and the excess of zeal to stand in his way. When it came to dealing with a human being, he dealt with him as God had made him to be. And when our own violation of man-made rules and regulations comes from that source, and with that attitude, then we will act as Jesus did. May God help us to have the wisdom and the courage to do so.

6

False Forces

Now we come to the third natural division of the first half of Mark's wonderful picture of the Servant who rules and the Ruler who serves. We have seen that the first division describes the authority of the servant—the tremendous command Jesus exercised in many realms. The second division brought before us his knowledge of our humanity—his penetrating, incisive understanding of man. The third of these natural divisions extends from chapter 3, verse 7 to chapter 6, verse 6. Its theme is underscored by the emphasis on the crowds which followed Jesus. This is the period of high popularity in our Lord's ministry:

> Jesus withdrew with his disciples to the sea, and a great multitude from Galilee followed; also from Judea and Jerusalem and Idumea and from beyond the Jordan and from about Tyre and Sidon a great multitude, hearing all that he did, came to him (Mk. 3:7–8).

I think we have difficulty grasping the size of this crowd. This was not just a few people, or a few thousand. There were literally tens of thousands of people, undoubtedly, in this crowd. They came from all over the country—from Galilee, from Judea, which began fifty miles to the south, from Jerusalem, the capital of Judea some seventy miles south of the Sea of Galilee, and beyond that from the land of Idumea, or Edom, way down in the southern desert, and from the region east of the Jordan River stretching out into the Arabian Desert, and from the west to the Mediterranean coast and up the coast to Tyre and Sidon, the area now in the country of Lebanon. They flocked out from all the cities to hear this amazing prophet who had risen in Galilee and was saying such startling things.

You can see how Mark traces the emphasis upon the crowd throughout this division. In verse 20 he says: ". . . and the crowd came together again, so that they could not even eat." Then in verse 32: ". . . a crowd was sitting about him . . ." And in chapter 4, verse 1: "Again he began to teach beside the sea. And a very large crowd gathered about him . . ." And then in verse 36 Mark says, "And leaving the crowd" they went across to the other side of the lake. In chapter 5, verse 21: "And when Jesus had crossed again in the boat to the other side, a great crowd gathered about him . . ." And in verse 24: "And a great crowd followed him and thronged about him." So this is the period when Jesus is pressed by the great masses of people, the period of his greatest popularity.

For many, this has been the symbol of Jesus' success, as it would be for many in evaluating a person today. Anybody who can get a great crowd following him is regarded as a success. We have all kinds of people who do that. We call them "stars" —there are star actors, star athletes, star singers, star politicians, people who have attained what in our day is a mark of success. No wonder the title of one of today's most popular musicals is *Jesus Christ, Superstar*. He is the One who drew all these great multitudes out from the cities of his day.

But as you read this account through, you see that Mark's intention is to underscore the weakness of popularity, the empty,

hollow worthlessness of being popular, and how much damage
and danger popularity produced in our Lord's ministry. There
are six ways this is brought out in this division. We will take
only the first of them in this study, from chapter 3, verse 7, to
the end of the chapter: The false and always hindering effects
which are invariably produced when a movement becomes
popular. They are a warning for us. Popularity produced them
in the days of Jesus, and popularity produces them today. Mark
gives us three illustrations of this danger, the first of which is
found in verses 9 and 10. After describing the crowd he says,

> And he told his disciples to have a boat ready for him because
> of the crowd, lest they should crush him; for he had healed
> many, so that all who had diseases pressed upon him to touch
> him (Mk. 3:9–10).

This underscores certain unwanted and misplaced emphases
which were made by this crowd. They misunderstood the purpose for which Jesus came, and they began to emphasize that
which was secondary in his thinking. You see this all through
the ministry of Jesus, especially with regard to the healing of
physical bodies.

But That's Not the Point!

Now, our Lord did heal physically. There is no question
about it. But from that day to this, men have seized upon that
as though it were preeminently the thing he came to do. Yet as
you read the Gospels carefully, you see that Jesus is very careful
to play it down and to emphasize that he came to heal the
spirits of men and not their bodies. He healed their bodies in
order to demonstrate what he could do and would do in the
realm of the Spirit.

For this is the way we are made. Human nature is such that
what is going on internally must become externalized. It must
show up in something which affects our bodies. We well know

that if we are anxious or troubled or upset it can result, if long continued, in certain physical defects. We can develop a nervous tic or twitch or can get ulcers—all kinds of things can go wrong because of some malady in our inner man.

Thus, Jesus healed the body to demonstrate what he could do with the spirit. But the crowd misunderstood that, and they pressed around him so that he might touch those who were sick and heal them—so much so that our Lord had to resort to a stratagem to avoid being crushed, literally, by this crowd. That is how large it was.

The interesting thing is that the device he used to get away was perfectly human. Notice that Jesus didn't play with magic here. He didn't build an invisible barrier around himself so that nobody could get close, or step into a phone booth, change clothes, and then leap into the sky. He is human. And in order to escape he asks his disciples to keep a boat handy on the shore so that he can step into it and move out onto the lake where the crowd can't follow him—in order that he might preach instead of heal.

All they wanted was healing. He wanted to preach. This is one of the things popularity does. It invariably distorts a message and emphasizes something secondary, which becomes paramount in the eyes of the people so that they miss the point.

The second false force popularity awakens is given in verse 11:

And whenever the unclean spirits beheld him, they fell down before him and cried out, "You are the Son of God." And he strictly ordered them not to make him known (Mk. 3:11–12).

Behind these diseases, the Scriptures tell us, were often the presence and the power of unclean spirits. Have you noticed how many times in Scripture these demons are called "unclean"? In this day when we are seeing such an upsurge of demonic activity, we need to understand this, because it is one of the ways you can recognize the presence of a demon. It is unclean—either morally or physically.

A friend told me of dealing years ago with a man who had an unclean spirit. As they talked in a hotel room in Portland, this man placed his hat on the bed. When he left, my friend found a ring of foul smelling grease where his hat had been. The odor pervaded the room for days—evidence of the uncleanness of that spirit.

I remember talking with a girl who had fallen into the practice of using a Ouija board. It eventuated in her hearing voices that demanded she write things down before she could sleep at night. Invariably, what she had to write was moral filth—obscenities, ugly, evil words. Sometimes she would have to write pages of them before the voices would cease and she could sleep. This is a mark of the kind of spirits these were.

Rejected Testimony

Mark tells us that when they saw Jesus, they always identified him. They cried out, "You are the Son of God." And Jesus invariably silenced them and cast them out. Why do you suppose he rejected this testimony from these demonic entities? You remember that when Paul and Barnabas were in Philippi, a young girl followed them and cried out something similar: "These men are servants of the most high God." They refused that witness. Paul finally cast the demon out of the young girl. So, everywhere in the Scriptures you find both the Lord and the apostles rejecting this kind of testimony. Yet it was true. He *was* the Son of God. But Jesus would not permit that witness to come from these demons. What was his reason for that?

Well, we can be sure of one thing—these unclean spirits did not desire to advance the cause of Christ by their witness. They told the truth, but they did so because they knew it would hurt the cause of Jesus, not help it. They were out to mislead people about Christ. So something about the way they told this, though it was true, was nevertheless misleading, and that is what our Lord rejected.

Some commentators suggest that because they were known to be "lying spirits" their testimony that Jesus *was* the Son of God would be construed as proof that he *wasn't*. In Mark Twain's fascinating book about his travels in the West and in Hawaii, *Roughing It,* there is an account of a man who was a notorious liar, who was known in the community to be a spinner of tall tales. No one ever believed anything he said. One day they found him hanging dead, with a suicide note pinned on him which said that he had taken his own life. But the coroner's jury pronounced it murder. They said that if the man himself said he had taken his own life, it was proof he hadn't!

But it is more likely that these demons intended that men would believe he was the son of the god whom they worshiped, i.e., Satan himself. When they said, "He is the Son of God," people would associate Jesus with demonic beings and with the devil himself. Therefore, it is no accident that in just two more paragraphs you read of a delegation coming from Jerusalem who accuse Jesus of being possessed by a devil. That is why Jesus totally rejected this witness from the underworld that he was the Son of God.

Selected Witnesses

The answer of our Lord to this threat is given in verses 13 through 19:

And he went up into the hills, and called to him those whom he desired; and they came to him. And he appointed twelve, to be with him, and to be sent out to preach and have authority to cast out demons: Simon whom he surnamed Peter; James the son of Zebedee and John the brother of James, whom he surnamed Boanerges, that is, sons of thunder; Andrew, and Philip, and Bartholomew, and Matthew, and Thomas, and James the son of Alphaeus, and Thaddaeus, and Simon the Canaanean, and Judas Iscariot, who betrayed him (Mk. 3:13–19).

These are the twelve whom Jesus selected. It is evident in the contrast between this paragraph and the previous one that Mark wants us to understand that the witness Jesus wanted was not pretentious claims and impressive titles from demons, true as they might have been, but rather he wanted the witness of changed lives and empowered words, of men who had been with him and whose lives were different as a result, who were sent out to say what they had heard and learned, and who, therefore, had power to speak authoritatively—even over the demons. This was the witness he chose. It is the witness he chooses yet today.

Notice that these twelve men were called to do three things. They were called to a *personal experience* first—to be with him. Jesus never wants anybody to talk about Christianity as an advocate, but always as a witness, i.e., telling of something which has happened to you. If you are merely a salesman on behalf of Christianity, holding it up to be a very fine approach to life or a great moral teaching, then you are an ineffective witness. The Lord doesn't want that. He wants a witness who has had something happen to him.

Then they were sent out for *purposeful evangelism.* They were sent out to preach, to say what they had learned from him. And they were given a *powerful exorcism*—they were to cast out demons. That is, they were given something to say, they were sent out to say it, and they were given power over all the opposition.

It is extremely interesting that in order to reach the multitudes our Lord selected only twelve men. That is the way to do it. We often make a great mistake in our day by relying too heavily on mass media. We think we are going to reach the multitudes through the great inventions which have come along—radio, television, cassette tapes, etc. As helpful as they are, nevertheless, they will not take the place of men and women who have had a personal experience with Christ and who tell it out in whatever way they can—perhaps even through some of these media—and who have obvious power in their life to overcome the enemy and to stand against all opposition. This is the witness our Lord has chosen.

The twelve disciples are listed for us here and their names are familiar. Simon, James, and John are first, and they are all given special names by Jesus. He "surnamed" them, i.e., he chose other names for them. This marks them as belonging to an inner circle within the twelve. You remember how frequently we read after this that when Jesus went to do something special, he took with him Peter and James and John. He dealt more intimately with these three than he did with any of the others. Thereby, he designated them leaders of this group, the means by which the others would be reached, in that remarkable method which both the Lord and the apostles employed of reaching the few in order to reach the many.

Peter he called the "rock"; James and John he called the "sons of thunder." It is instructive to me that when he looked at this group of twelve men, what he saw as being needed in this band was a rock and two loud voices. Peter was the acknowledged leader of the twelve and was the one who ultimately proved to be the rock, the steady one to whom the others looked for leadership and upon whom they relied for guidance. James left his mark by laying down his life first among the twelve, and John remained until the end to gather up all the apostolic witness, solidify it, and transmit it to us in its final expression in the Gospel of John, the Letters of John, and the Book of Revelation. So this was the leadership within the twelve, and our Lord dealt with them so that they might be the witness which ultimately would reach not only the multitudes there at hand but eventually all the world. Jesus was content to work with these.

The third example of falseness arising out of popularity is given to us beginning with the latter part of verse 19:

> Then he went home; and the crowd came together again, so that they could not even eat. And when his friends heard it, they went out to seize him, for they said, "He is beside himself." And the scribes who came down from Jerusalem said, "He is possessed by Beelzebul, and by the prince of demons he casts out the demons" (Mk. 3:19–22).

Here are two reactions to Jesus, to the intensity of his ministry. He gave himself so totally to this ministry, to these crowds, that he had no time even to eat. His friends heard about this and were disturbed. The word translated "friends" really means "relatives"—literally, "those from beside him." We learn from the latter part of the chapter that it is actually his mother and his brothers. They are up in Nazareth and word reaches them that he is not taking care of himself. He is not eating properly. He is not sleeping properly. His health is threatened. So they leave Nazareth and come to try to put him under restraint. Their feeling is that he has gone crazy, that he is "beside himself"—literally, "outside himself"—as a result of his concern for the hurt of the world. Jesus will handle that misapprehension at the end of this account.

Satanic Godfather

But first he deals with the accusations of the scribes who came down from Jerusalem and who watched this same activity. Their explanation was, "He is possessed by the devil, by Beelzebul." Beelzebul means "lord of the house." It is a reference to Satan as king of the underworld, head of the demonic "Mafia," if you like. Beelzebul was the "godfather" who gave the orders, and the rest of the demons all followed. The scribes' explanation of the ministry of Jesus was that he was in league with demons, that he had joined the Mafia and was casting out these demons by the power of the satanic godfather. Jesus answers with very simple logic:

And he called them to him, and said to them in parables, "How can Satan cast out Satan? If a kingdom is divided against itself, that kingdom cannot stand. And if a house is divided against itself [Remember Beelzebul means the "lord of the house"], that house will not be able to stand. And if Satan has risen up against himself and is divided, he cannot stand, but is coming to an end (Mk. 3:23–26).

That is clear argument, isn't it? Satan, Jesus suggests, is clever and resourceful. He would never oppose himself by using Jesus to cast out demons. That would create anarchy in the underworld. It would polarize his whole kingdom and create division and strife among his minions, and Satan would never permit that. He rules by fear. The satanic kingdom knows nothing of love or loyalty. It is fear, abject terror, which controls it. Satan would never have permitted this kind of revolutionary activity within his kingdom. Jesus knows this and points it out to the scribes. And he says, "No, something else has happened." Then he describes what really is happening: "But no one can enter a strong man's house and plunder his goods, unless he first binds the strong man; then indeed he may plunder his house" (Mk. 3:27).

This is what has happened. Jesus is the stronger man and has entered the house of Satan and bound him. Today, we frequently hear about people who go around "binding" Satan. But I submit that this is totally unnecessary. There is only One who can bind the devil. And he has already done it. Jesus bound the devil even in the days of his ministry and thus made it possible for himself to cast out these unclean spirits and to plunder the house of Satan and release those he had held captive for so long—humanity. This is the explanation of what has hap-

pened. So today we don't need to go about binding the devil.
We may properly exercise the authority to cast out evil spirits.
But it is because the devil is already bound that we have that
possibility at all. And it is only One who has made that possible—the Lord Jesus himself.

Having answered that claim, he now moves on to issue a very
severe warning to these scribes:

> "Truly, I say to you, all sins will be forgiven the sons of men,
> and whatever blasphemies they utter; but whoever blasphemes
> against the Holy Spirit never has forgiveness, but is guilty of
> an eternal sin"—for they had said, "He has an unclean spirit"
> (Mk. 3:28–30).

Many have been very frightened by that paragraph, and
rightly so. It is a serious word that Jesus uttered. Some have
concluded from it that the unpardonable sin is suggesting that
Jesus had an unclean spirit, or that the works of God are really
the works of the devil. But it is important to notice certain
things about this account. Notice that these men had not yet
committed the unpardonable sin when they said Jesus had an
unclean spirit. Otherwise Jesus would never have warned them.
By his own words, there is no use warning a man who has committed the unpardonable sin; he is beyond help. He cannot be
forgiven. So if that is what these men had done, there would
have been no point to his warning.

Rejecting the Spirit's Witness

But he *did* warn them, so it is clear that they had not yet
committed it. But they are on the verge of it. They are close to
it. "You are very close to committing that sin," Jesus says,
"when you ascribe the work of God to the devil." That is very
close. What Jesus warned them against was rejecting the witness of the Holy Spirit. And to whom does the Spirit witness?
Well, all through the Scriptures the Holy Spirit is given to

witness to the Lord Jesus. "He has come to bear witness to me," Jesus said later on to his disciples, "and he will take of the things of *mine* and make them known unto you. . . . He came into the world to convict men of sin . . . because they believe not on me." All the work of the Holy Spirit is designed to exalt and declare and define the work of Jesus. So to reject the Holy Spirit, to blaspheme the Holy Spirit, is to reject the Spirit's witness of Christ.

That is what these men were close to doing. And it is true, therefore, that if in the ultimate there is a rejection of Christ, then there is no hope, because there is no ground of forgiveness other than faith in the Lord Jesus. Men are forgiven when they believe in his name—and on no other basis. If that is set aside, ultimately and finally—this is not a single act of rejection which is in view, it is a process—if the heart is resistant and rejects the claims of Jesus as set forth by the Holy Spirit, the result is that there can be no forgiveness. This is Scripture's sharp way of underscoring the fact which Jesus himself declared, "No man comes unto the Father but by me."

Having said this, our Lord deals with the misunderstanding of his relatives:

And his mother and his brothers came; and standing outside they sent to him and called him. And a crowd was sitting about him; and they said to him, "Your mother and your brothers are outside, asking for you." And he replied, "Who are my mother and my brothers?" And looking around on those who sat about him, he said, "Here are my mother and my brothers! Whoever does the will of God is my brother, and sister, and mother" (Mk. 3:31–35).

When word was brought in that Jesus' mother and brothers were outside, everybody expected him immediately to go out and see them. But Jesus didn't—deliberately. Instead he looked around and said these strange words: "Here are my mother and my brothers and sisters. Everyone who does the will of God is closer to me than they."

A Stronger Tie

Was he beside himself because he seemingly neglected his family and himself? No, he was simply possessed and held by a stronger tie. Dearer even than his own earthly family were those who were his brothers and sisters and his mother in the family of God. Thus he makes clear that there is a primacy of relationship in which those ties that bind us to our brothers and sisters in Christ, and to the Lord Jesus and to God our Father, are stronger and make more imperious demands upon us than those of our own natural family.

I want to say a word of caution about an idea which is being circulated widely these days. I don't want to attack it, particularly, because there is much truth in it. But I want to raise a warning which grows out of this incident in our Lord's experience. There is a teaching abroad which says that a Christian is bound by the authority of his father and mother almost throughout his life. It is called by several names, like the "Chain of Command," or the "Chain of Counsel." Now, there is a great deal of truth in it, because it recognizes relationships which are important—especially as children are growing up. And respect and honor are always to be given to those who are our kin by natural ties. Our Lord Jesus never instructed a person to ignore his responsibilities to his natural kin—never. In fact, the Scriptures make clear that, as Paul puts it, a man who doesn't care for his own is worse than an infidel. Jesus also pointed out how wrong the Pharisees were in using the law to evade their responsibilities to their parents.

But what our Lord does point out very clearly here is that when there is a conflict between what God says, the demands of God in our life, and the advice and counsel of our relatives according to the flesh, it is the Word of God which has primacy. It must be the deciding factor in our life. And though we are responsible to declare our decision with love and compassion and understanding, we must follow what God says. This is why Jesus said clearly and repeatedly, "If a man forsakes not his father and his mother, and his wife and his children, and himself, and even all that he has, he cannot be my disciple." He makes that supreme claim upon us, having fulfilled it himself. And this is why on fairly numerous occasions he himself seems to ignore his ties with his mother and his brothers and sisters in order that he might be faithful to the calling of God.

One of the worst things that can happen to us, as this account makes clear, is to become caught up in a popular movement. False forces arise out of it. That is the whole thrust of this section. Misemphases easily spring into being and wrongful attitudes arise readily in a popular movement. Popularity, therefore, ought to be watched very carefully. And when a movement is popular, as Christianity is popular in many places today, we must be very careful that we are listening to the voice and the Spirit of God.

7

The Dimming of the Light

Now we come to the section in which Mark describes how and why Jesus began to use the parabolic method of teaching. A parable is a little story which illustrates a truth. It is a vocal cartoon. We all appreciate cartoons because they drive a point home in a very striking way. Not long ago, I visited a pastor who had plastered one whole wall of his study with cartoons—some of them funny! I like cartoons myself. My wife gave me one the other day which shows an old man, bald-headed and hook-nosed, standing up in the middle of a congregation and saying, "I've just received a message direct from the Lord. He says he's sick to death with guitar music and tambourines!" Now, that does not represent my point of view, but I appreciate the humor of it because it drives a point home. That is what a parable is like, and this is the method Jesus began to use.

But a parable is also a slight dimming of the light, a kind of hiding of the truth. Because of his popularity, Jesus found it necessary to change his approach from the direct and literal to the symbolic method, so as to hide the truth a bit. Mark introduces the theme to us in chapter 4:

Again he began to teach beside the sea. And a very large crowd gathered about him, so that he got into a boat and sat in it on the sea; and the whole crowd was beside the sea on the land. And he taught them many things in parables . . . (Mk. 4: 1–2).

This opening description takes us back to chapter 3, where Jesus told his disciples to have a boat ready for him because of the crowd. Mark tells us here that the crowd pressed him so much that he had to get into the boat. Thus they defeated their own purpose by pressing him so on this matter of healing. Jesus made use of his emergency preparation, got into the boat, withdrew from the crowd, and began to teach them.

But he taught in a way he never had before; he began to tell them stories, parables. This is the first occasion Jesus ever made use of a parable. He did speak to them before in parabolic statements (brief figures of speech) but not in full-fledged story form. It was the parable of the sower, and all the Gospel writers agree that this was the first one he had ever told. The disciples were impressed by this story and by the way Jesus told it, and they asked him about it later. Let us read the story he told:

. . . and in his teaching he said to them: "Listen! A sower went out to sow. And as he sowed, some seed fell along the path, and the birds came and devoured it. Other seed fell on rocky ground, where it had not much soil, and immediately it sprang up, since it had no depth of soil; and when the sun rose it was scorched, and since it had no root it withered away. Other seed fell among thorns and the thorns grew up and choked it, and it yielded no grain. And other seeds fell into good soil and brought forth grain, growing up and increasing and yielding thirtyfold and sixtyfold and a hundredfold." And he said, "He who has ears to hear, let him hear" (Mk. 4:2–9).

This parable of the sower and the soils is linked in this section with two other stories of seeds. There is the seed growing secretly, in verses 26 and on, followed immediately by the story of the mustard seed which grew into a great plant. For now, however, I want to focus on what immediately follows the story of the sower because the disciples were curious as to why Jesus used parables. I would like to face this problem directly, since Mark gives us the explanation from the lips of Jesus himself. Why did he turn to the use of parables and never turn back from it from this time on? Well, we have an explanatory paragraph beginning in verse 10:

> And when he was alone, those who were about him with the twelve asked him concerning the parables. And he said to them, "To you has been given the secret of the kingdom of God, but for those outside everything is in parables; so that they may indeed see but not perceive, and may indeed hear but not understand; lest they should turn again, and be forgiven" (Mk. 4:10–12).

That latter verse has caused a great deal of difficulty in many people's minds. What did he mean? Did he actually mean that he spoke in parables in order to hide the truth so that people could not understand it and thereby be forgiven? It sounds as though this is what he said. But this is only one of three explanatory paragraphs Mark gives us in which Jesus himself helps us to understand the reasons why he spoke in parables.

In this first one, the Lord points out that there are two kinds of hearers, and that this is why he speaks in parables: "To you has been given the secret of the kingdom of God." That is one class of hearers—the disciples of Jesus—those who follow him, who are obedient to him, who listen to him and accept his authority as Lord and teacher. To them is given the *secret* of the kingdom of God.

Sacred Secrets . . .

The word he actually uses is "mystery"—"the *mystery* of the kingdom of God." I am always entranced by these mysteries which are mentioned in Scripture. They are not vague and difficult to understand; the word does not mean that. But they are secret from the majority of people. Paul, in 1 Corinthians, says of the apostles, "This is how one should regard us, as servants of Christ and stewards of the mysteries of God." That is, as men entrusted with sacred secrets which God has told to men.

What are these mysteries? Basically, as you read through the Scriptures, you see that they are inside information on life which only believers, only disciples, are given to understand. They are, in fact, truths which the natural man cannot discover by himself. Here is the world and all humanity, working away trying to explain what we are, to understand the universe in which we live, and the society in which we function—how it works and why it embodies such difficult problems. The nuclear physicist comes along and puts in a piece of the puzzle. Then along comes the geologist and he fits in a piece. Then the psychologist and psychiatrist fill out a part of it, and we begin to understand a bit more. Then the philosophers add their part. We keep working away at putting together this tremendously complex, amazing jigsaw puzzle of life, trying to understand it.

. . . Missing Pieces

But Jesus declares here that there are certain missing pieces which only God can put in. And they are essential to the understanding of the problem! These he calls "the mysteries of God." In chapters 1 and 2 of 1 Corinthians, Paul describes them as the "deep things" of God. He says the natural man cannot understand them, for they are revealed only by the Spirit of God: "For what person knows a man's thoughts except the spirit of the man which is in him? So also no one comprehends the thoughts of God except the Spirit of God." Only the Spirit of God knows these deep things of God, these great and enlightening secrets which help you to grasp fully what is going on in your life or in anybody else's. Therefore, this is not merely theological hogwash. This is practical truth which is hidden from us and can be revealed only by God himself.

Scripture speaks of various mysteries. In 2 Thessalonians

Paul speaks of the "mystery of lawlessness." This is what men all around us are trying to solve today—the reason why evil persists in human hearts, why there seems to be a fountain of evil and violence in man which, no matter what we do to treat the symptoms, continues to pour out ever-increasing manifestations of violence and bitterness and hatred and prejudice and persecution. This is where educators, legislators, and social planners wrestle. Why is all this true? The revelation which explains it is in the secrets God alone reveals. That is why more than anything else we need to understand the Bible, because it holds the key to the problems which are at work in our lives.

Then Paul speaks of the "mystery of godliness"—the counterpart of the mystery of lawlessness. This is the secret of how to cope with life, how to handle these problems of violence and evil which you find even within yourself, how to handle pressures and disasters, perplexities, and all the common irritations which come our way, how to react to them, what to do about them so that you can handle everything which comes and remain calm and poised and at peace and effective in the lives of others. That is the mystery of godliness, or Godlikeness, which is the full meaning of the word.

But here Mark speaks of the mystery of the kingdom. What does this mean? It means the understanding of what God is doing now in history—how the events of our day are being used in the program and planning of God, God's rule over men at work in current events. This is the mystery of the kingdom— how God functions in human society, just exactly what he is doing today, and how he is doing it. The world would have us believe that everything takes place quite apart from God, that if there is a God he is sitting up there some place watching us poor, struggling mortals down here on the sinful plains of life, but that he really has nothing to do with it; he is just watching it happen. The Scriptures, though, reveal that God himself is involved in every single event, that nothing occurs which God is not in touch with and has not arranged and brought into

being. Without destroying our will to choose or our freedom to
move, he, nevertheless, is working things out to a vast and
cosmic purpose which he announces to us. That is the mystery
of the kingdom of God. "And to you," Jesus says, "you who are
disciples, is given that secret. You can understand it."

But there is a second class, described as "those outside." For
those outside everything is in parables. Who are these? Well,
of course, they are everyone who is not a disciple. There are
many church members or regular church attenders who are not
really disciples, not really open to understanding and obeying
the Lordship of Christ (which is what a disciple must be), and
so the truth is hidden from them. To them the parables will be
simple stories without much meaning.

Jesus then said this rather solemn, amazing thing: ". . . everything is in parables; so that they may indeed see but *not*
perceive, and may indeed hear but *not* understand; *lest* they
should turn again, and be forgiven." This is the part which
troubles many. It does indeed sound as though Jesus is saying,
"I don't want them to turn again. I've hidden this truth so that
they won't. The last thing I want is for them to be forgiven."
But we know immediately that is not true; that cannot be what
this means.

We will be helped greatly if we understand two things about
this account. One is that it is highly condensed, Mark's account
of this statement is the most condensed of all. We need the
parallel passages in Matthew and Luke as well, particularly in
Matthew, to understand what Jesus is saying here, and we will
look at these in a moment.

It Is Fulfilled

The second thing we need to understand is that this is a
poorly edited account. The editors have failed us at this point.
It would help a great deal if you would take pencil or pen and
put some additional quotation marks around these words:
" '. . . they may indeed see but not perceive, and may indeed

hear but not understand; lest they should turn again, and be forgiven.' " Jesus is not originating this statement; he is quoting Isaiah. He is saying that this word of Isaiah is being fulfilled at the present time. He does not say, "I'm speaking in parables in *order* that it might be fulfilled"; he is saying, "I'm speaking in parables *because* it is being fulfilled." That makes a big difference. It would be perfectly valid for you to insert the words "it is fulfilled" in verse 12: ". . . so that *it is fulfilled,* 'they may indeed see but not perceive, and may indeed hear but not understand; lest they should turn again, and be forgiven.' " If you look at Matthew 13:14, you see that this is exactly what has happened. In this parallel passage, the full quotation from Isaiah is given to us: "With them indeed is fulfilled the prophecy of Isaiah which says: 'You shall indeed hear but never understand, and you shall indeed see but never perceive' " (vs. 14). Then Isaiah goes on to explain why this is happening. Mark leaves this out and quotes only the conclusion. But in Matthew 13:15, we have the explanation from Isaiah: " 'For this people's heart has grown dull, and their ears are heavy of hearing, and their eyes they have closed . . .' "

Who closed their eyes? Not God. The *people* closed them. And why did they close their eyes? " '. . . lest they should perceive with their eyes, and hear with their ears, and understand with their heart, and turn for me to heal them' " (Matt. 13:14–15).

The people did not want to be healed. That is the point. In order to prevent the healing of their spirit, of the hurt of their heart, which Jesus wanted to bring them, they closed their eyes and ears. What did the people want? They wanted physical healing, and that is all they wanted. They wanted Jesus to cure their diseases and get rid of all their afflictions so they could go on just as they were before. Jesus, knowing this, tells them, "You are fulfilling the very words of Isaiah the prophet, in that you are not willing to listen to what I have to say. You want me to heal only the body."

So, to capture their attention, Jesus said in effect: "I'll tell you the truth in parables. If you won't listen to this teaching, then I'll give it to you in a different way"—in order that he might reach them. This gives us a clear understanding of what he is saying here in Mark—that parables are designed for the uninterested, for those who have turned their minds off. This is his first explanation—that there are two classes of hearers.

Immediately there follows the explanation of the parable of the sower and the soils, which we will reserve for the next chapter. Let's skip to the paragraph beginning with Mark 4:21, and notice the second reason Jesus gives for his use of parables:

> And he said to them, "Is a lamp brought in to be put under a bushel, or under a bed, and not on a stand? For there is nothing hid, except to be made manifest; nor is anything secret, except to come to light. If any man has ears to hear, let him hear." And he said to them, "Take heed what you hear; the measure you give will be the measure you get, and still more will be given to you. For to him who has will more be given; and from him who has not, even what he has will be taken away" (Mk. 4:21–25).

In that paragraph there are three principles for understanding how parables work. The first is given in verses 21 and 22: "Is a lamp brought in to be put under a bushel, or under a bed, and not on a stand?" Of course not! If a man brings a lamp into a house, he puts it on a stand; he doesn't hide it. Notice that Jesus is still talking about why he speaks in parables. He says, "For there is nothing hid (and a parable is a way of hiding truth), except to be made manifest; nor is anything secret, except to come to light." In other words, to put it plainly, hiding makes truth more visible. That is an amazing paradox, but true. If you hide the truth slightly, it makes it even easier to see.

Every morning when I get up I stand in front of a mirror—not to admire what I see, which is very discouraging—but in order to shave. My mirror has two lights, one on either side,

capable of yielding two different intensities of light: very
bright, and dim. Long ago I learned that if I turned the lights
on bright, they would shine so intensely into my eyes that I
could not see my face. The only way I can shave successfully
is to dim the lights—then I can see what I am doing. When the
light is dimmer, my face is easier to see. That is an illustration
of what Jesus is saying here.

In Proverbs 25:2 you find this great teaching: "It is the
glory of God to conceal a thing, but the glory of kings is to
search it out." God loves to conceal truth. And we like it, too.
We are all intrigued by mystery, by things cryptic and hidden.
We love to search them out. God appeals to this in human
nature and hides truth from us. But it is only to make it more
visible. He does this in nature. How much truth God has hidden away in the world of nature all around us! Through the
centuries men have puzzled, thought, scratched their heads, and
tried various approaches as they have worked on finding it. As
they gradually have begun to understand something about it,
that truth discovered has changed the whole course of life. God
hid it in order that men might find it.

Hidden in a Man

He did the same thing with Jesus himself. The Gospel of
John tells us that "the Word became flesh and dwelt among
us"—God reduced to a man. If we suddenly saw God in all his
splendor, we would be absolutely pulverized. But the glory of
God, so bright and brilliant that no human creature can stand
in its presence, was hidden in a man, in Jesus. John says, "We
have beheld his glory, glory as of the only begotten of the
Father, full of grace and truth." Grace and truth—the two
things which glorify God. But men could never have seen this
glory if it had not been hidden in the life of Jesus.

Understanding this principle, Jesus knew that men would
grasp the truth more readily if he hid it in a parable. And men
know this, too. One of the ancient philosophers, the Stoic

Epictetus, wanted to teach his disciples a truth everyone needs to learn: that truth understood is of no value; it is truth acted upon which changes things. That is a great truth. But you can say that to people and it seems to run right off their backs. Sometimes we try putting it in a little epigram, like "Practice what you preach." That says the same thing, but in a little more graphic way. But I think the old philosopher did it best, for he taught it this way: He gathered his disciples around and said, "Have you ever noticed that a sheep does not vomit up the grass it ate at the feet of the shepherd in order to impress him. The sheep digests it to produce wool and milk." That is a vivid way of illustrating that truth, is it not? One you are not likely to forget! And that is what parables are—ways of putting truth succinctly and compellingly and accurately in ways you will not forget. That is why Jesus resorted to parables—because men's hearts had turned away and needed to be recaptured, brought to attention. The first principle, then, is that hiding makes truth more visible.

More Than You Expect

In Mark 4:24 Jesus reveals another principle: "And he said to them, 'Take heed what you hear; the measure you give will be the measure you get, and still more will be given to you.' " What does he mean by that? He means that in searching for truth you will discover far more than you expected to find. That is a principle on which to act. To parody the superlative "theologian," Dr. Flip Wilson, "What you seek is what you get—plus!" Plus more—". . . and still more will be given to you," Jesus said. You cannot get it apart from seeking. If you do not want to search the Word of God and seek the truth and think about it—forget it! It will not mean a thing to you. Your Bible will be as dull and deadly as any book could possibly be. And so it is for many, many people. But if you are willing to look, if you want to search, and ask, and pray, and seek, then God will give you what you are looking for. In searching, you will find—and more than you expected to find. I know that is true. I have seen it happen hundreds and hundreds of times as people have begun to seek out the truth.

The third principle is found in Mark 4:25: "For to him who has will more be given; and from him who has not, even what he has will be taken away." "But that's not fair," you say. It may not be, but that is the way life is. That is a basic rule of life: If you do not use what you have, you lose it. It is true on all levels. If you bind up your arm so that you cannot move it for as little as two weeks, when you remove the binding, you find you have temporarily lost the use of your arm. You have to work on it for a time before you are able to use it again. If you do not use your brain to reason and to think things through, you lose the ability. Life then becomes very shallow, and you see no depth in anything. You are caught up with the emotion of the moment, moving from one feeling to another. If you do not seize an opportunity that is given, you lose it. ". . . from him who has not, even what he has will be taken away." That is a principle of life. That is why Jesus spoke in parables— because these things are true. If you search, you will find truth you could not see otherwise, and more than you expected. If you do not search, you find that you have lost even the truth you once thought you had.

We will skip over the parables of the growing grain and the mustard seed for now and move on to verses 33 and 34, where our Lord concludes his explanation of why he spoke in parables:

> With many such parables he spoke the word to them, as they were able to hear it; he did not speak to them without a parable, but privately to his own disciples he explained everything (Mk. 4:33–34).

There again are the two classes of hearers. And there is also here one great rule of revelation given in these words: "as they were able to hear it." On another occasion he said to his disciples, "I have yet many things to say to you, but you cannot bear them now." Jesus teaches men only as they can take it. This is the rule upon which God works with us. He does not show us everything at once. If he did, he would destroy us.

The glory and wonder of the Scriptures is that they are put together in such an amazing way that it takes both the Word *and* the Spirit to understand the Bible. You can read the Word, and if you are not ready for it and open to it, those words will not say a thing to you. But if you are open, you will learn something from them. The next time you can come back, read the same words, and learn something more . . . and again and again. Each time you will learn something more. It never ceases to refresh your spirit, instruct your mind, and open and expand your capacity to receive from God. That is the way God teaches us truth as we are able to bear it.

Merciful Revelations

And this is true also of his revelation to us about ourselves. One of the great things about Scripture is that it shows you who you are and who you have been all along. God is gracious to us that way. He does not just rip the veil off so that suddenly you see the whole ghastly thing. If he did, we would be wiped out, absolutely wiped out. But he lifts it little by little. You shake and tremble and say, "Is *that* the way I've been?" You are aghast at the way you have been treating people, and you think, "Thank God that's over!" The next week he lifts it a little higher. You shake and tremble and go through it again, and say, "At last we've got to the bottom!" Then God lifts it high enough for you to see more, and you are wiped out again. But you handle it little by little. Because, along with the revelation of yourself, he also reveals himself and his adequacy to handle it. So gradually you begin to see what you have been all along—as you are able to bear it. This is the way God works.

This is why he hides truth from us, why it takes a long time to understand the Scriptures, why you will spend the rest of your life studying them and never get through. This is the rule upon which Jesus acted. He explained things to them and taught them many, many things as they were able to bear it. Is it not wonderful that he understands us that way and deals with us like that? If he revealed the glories of heaven to us suddenly, every one of us would be running out to jump into the ocean, to get there as fast as possible. But he lifts the veil only a little at a time as we are able to bear it.

The most terrible thing I see happening today is that people with Bibles in their hands are going to churches where the Bible is taught, and yet never understanding the secrets of the kingdom of heaven—these vast truths which change your life —because they really are not open and obedient to them and are not willing to search and to seek and to find what God has hidden in his Word. May God encourage you to begin to seek out these great mysteries.

8

Seed Thoughts

Now we want to join the disciples in listening to Jesus explain what he calls the "secrets of the kingdom of God." These "mysteries of the kingdom," as they are often referred to in our Scriptures, are really vital truths about humanity which are not discoverable in secular studies. You cannot find these in any university curriculum, unless it is related to the Word of God. And yet they are very essential truths which we must know about ourselves, about life, and about the world in which we live in order to grow and fulfill our humanity.

We have already seen how Jesus began to speak to the people in parables because of a subtle change which had occurred in the crowd. As a result of our Lord's earlier ministry, they had heard of his wonder-working power, his healing ministry, and his mighty, marvelous words of deliverance. Word had spread throughout the whole land, and people had come from north, south, east, and west and gathered in Galilee to hear this amazing prophet. At first, Jesus was able to speak to them very clearly and forthrightly, making tremendous declarations about humanity. During this period he gave the message we call the "Sermon on the Mount," undoubtedly the greatest message ever delivered in the presence of men, anywhere, at any time. Jesus longed to open their eyes and minds and hearts even more fully.

But a change had taken place. Crowds were pressing upon him—not to hear the Word but to be healed of their diseases. These people had shut their minds, turned off their ears to the words Jesus spoke, and were intent only upon the deeds he performed. It was for this reason Jesus began to speak in parables. He said that he hid the truth so that people's curiosity would be awakened, and they would seek it out. He warned the people of a natural law which could be stated, "Use it, or lose it." If you do not obey truth, you will lose truth—not only that truth you are hearing, but some you think you have already grasped.

Furthermore, he said that as men began to search these parables and seek to understand them, they would see truth only as they were able to bear it. That is a remarkable revelation, revealing to us the radical character of Christianity. Christian truth—which basically is reality, things as they really are —is so different from the way we think things are that we can hardly bear to hear it. Standards of values, modes of behavior, and styles of living are so different, so completely opposite to what we learn in the world, that we resist them. We do not want to hear them. It is only gradually that God can lift the veil and let us see ourselves as we really are. So the principle of revelation is: "as we are able to bear it." In 1 Corinthians 3, Paul stated that principle to the Corinthians: "I fed you with milk, not solid food; for you were not ready for it; and even yet you are not ready . . ." This is the condition of our humanity.

Mark gives us only three of the parables our Lord spoke on that first day, but he refers to "many such," and Matthew records seven parables given on this occasion. Mark's three are the parables of the sower and the soils, of the seed growing secretly, and of the mustard seed. Each is a revelation of the invisible reign of God in human affairs. Jesus takes us behind the scenes in each one and shows us something about the way God acts in human life, thereby revealing some of these mysteries of the kingdom.

We do not need to guess at what these are. The point of each parable emerges clearly as we understand what Jesus has explained to us. The first, the parable of the sower, is intended to show us how the kingdom comes into human life, how our eyes are opened, what God is doing, and how this touches us and enters our hearts. The second, the parable of the seed growing secretly, shows us how the kingdom grows, what forces we can count upon to see to it that this knowledge of ourselves and of God is increasing. The last, the parable of the mustard seed, shows us a very surprising effect the kingdom will have in the world. Let us take these parables one by one, beginning at Mark 4:3:

> "Listen! A sower went out to sow. And as he sowed, some seed fell along the path, and the birds came and devoured it. Other seed fell on rocky ground, where it had not much soil, and immediately it sprang up, since it had no depth of soil; and when the sun rose it was scorched, and since it had no root it withered away. Other seed fell among thorns and the thorns grew up and choked it, and it yielded no grain. And other seeds fell into good soil and brought forth grain, growing up and increasing and yielding thirtyfold and sixtyfold and a hundredfold." And he said, "He who has ears to hear, let him hear" (Mk. 4:3–9).

This first of all parables is very typical of the power of Jesus to illustrate from nature. I am sure that something like what this parable describes was going on right before the eyes of the people. Jesus was standing by the lake, and the crowd was spread across the hillside. They could see the side of the next hill, along the curve of the lakeshore, where a sower was out in the fields sowing grain. And, seeking a way to illustrate what he wanted to convey, Jesus saw the sower, took his activity as his text, and told the story as the crowd watched it happening before their very eyes. They could see the seed falling on various kinds of soil and birds coming to pick up some of it. All of this dramatically vivid before them.

The Interpretive Key

When Jesus said, "He who has ears to hear, let him hear," he made it evident that this was much more than just a story. It was not meant merely to entertain them. That phrase is like a sign which says "THINK." But evidently they did not understand him. Even the twelve gathered afterward and said, "Explain the parable to us." So Jesus went on to explain the parable to the twelve, and to us. As he gave them the explanation, he said this amazing thing: "And he said to them, 'Do you not understand this parable? How then will you understand all the parables?' " (Mark 4:13).

That is a very, very important sentence, because he is telling us that this parable of the sower is the key to interpreting *all* the parables. Otherwise, these words are without meaning. It is very important that we notice this. If we do not, we will make the mistake of many commentators who simply make these parables mean whatever they want them to mean. They have ignored this clear statement of Jesus that the parable of the sower is the key to interpreting all the parables. In fact, many of the commentators make up their own rules of interpretation as they go along. But listen to the way Jesus interprets this parable, beginning with verse 14:

> "The sower sows the word. And these are the ones along the path, where the word is sown; when they hear, Satan immediately comes and takes away the word which is sown in them. [Satan is represented by the birds that came and ate the seed.] And these in like manner are the ones sown upon rocky ground, who, when they hear the word, immediately receive it

with joy; and they have no root in themselves, but endure for a while; then, when tribulation or persecution arises on account of the word, immediately they fall away. And others are the ones sown among thorns; they are those who hear the word, but the cares of the world, and the delight in riches, and the desire for other things, enter in and choke the word, and it proves unfruitful. But those that were sown upon the good soil are the ones who hear the word and accept it and bear fruit, thirtyfold and sixtyfold and a hundredfold" (Mk. 4:14–20).

Please notice that Jesus treats it exactly as some commentators say he must not do! He treats it as an allegory. He says every detail means something. And he says, furthermore, that this is the way to handle all the parables. This is the key to understanding parables. Parables are allegories in which every detail applies, has its own import to the whole. From that, I think we can deduce a very practical exhortation: as the song says, "Read your Bible. The words inside are true and reliable." And they throw a great deal of light on the commentaries!

A Magic Hour

Let us look at this story of the sower and see the first of these secrets of the kingdom—how the kingdom of God comes to us. Jesus says first that the sower goes out and sows, and the Word is what he sows. This is how the kingdom arrives in human hearts. The Word of God is sown by means of preaching or teaching or reading or studying or witnessing, or in some other way. The Word is dropped into hearts like seeds into soil. That Word is the life-giving element which can change the whole situation and bring enrichment and harvest into a life. Therefore, the moment of the sowing of the Word is a magic hour. It is a time when the opportunity to be changed is present.

I used to read this story as though these various soils were

four different kinds of people who remained the same all
through their lifetimes—some were permanently hard-hearted,
like the first example given; some were impulsive, like the
second; some were full of concerns, like the third, etc. But I
have come to see that what our Lord is describing here is not
types of persons, so much, but conditions of heart at any given
moment, i.e., conditions which are present when the Word is
being sown. Whenever the Word is being sown, people are in
one condition or another, just as they are described to us here.
We have all been callous, at times, when we have heard the
Word. We have all been impulsive in our reactions—emotional, shallow. We have all been overly concerned about
other matters. And we have all had times of being open and
responsive to the Word.

What is your heart like now? You are in one of these four
conditions. Which one? That is the question.

Let us look at them. First, there is what we can call the
callous heart. The seed is sown upon the beaten, trodden-down
pathway. This represents people whose hearts are busy, who
are not open, who have been beaten down so many times they
have grown cynical, hardhearted—callous to truth. When the
seed hits them, the birds come and gather it up immediately.
What does Jesus say about that kind of a life? He says it is
strictly for the birds! The seed will be snatched away by Satan
before you even have a chance to hear it.

C. S. Lewis, in his *Screwtape Letters,* describes a man who
goes into a library to read and meditate. His mind is suddenly
opened to deep thoughts of God. Confronted with his own
standing before God, he starts thinking in terms of his eternal
welfare. Then, Lewis says, the demons that are assigned to
keep him from discovering truth call his attention to the
sounds on the street, to the newsboy calling out the latest
news, and to the fact that he is hungry. And that is all it takes.
All thoughts of God disappear, and he is involved in the

mundane affairs of life. And, from the point of view of the satanic emissaries, he is delivered from his danger of thinking about God. That is what happens to the callous mind and heart.

Then there are the impulsive hearts. The seed falls upon them and they immediately respond with joy. The seed takes root and grows up quickly. The trouble is, they respond like this to everything—food fads, new books, political leaders, whatever popular movement happens to be abroad at the time. As a result, their lives are so shallow that the seed of the life-giving Word cannot take deep root and change them. Consequently, the life which apparently is there withers away and dies. Jesus says that this kind of life is shallow; it cannot stand the heat. When persecution and tribulation come, immediately it is withered. Such turn away and lose interest, and cannot abide.

Three Kinds of Thorns

The third condition of heart is represented by the thorns. These are those who hear the Word, but thorns spring up and choke it. This is what we could call the overinvolved heart. Jesus details three kinds of thorns that choke the life-giving Word. First, there are cares, i.e., worries, concerns. There are people who are concerned all the time over what is going to happen next, worried about the situation they are facing—fretful, anxious, troubled people who do not know how to rest, how to leave things in God's hands but are constantly trying to work it all out themselves. These people, Jesus says, are losing truth. The seed has fallen upon their hearts, but it does not take root because it is choked by the thorns and they soon lose it.

Second, there are those who delight in riches, who are caught up in the pursuit of wealth, in the Playboy philosophy—constantly planning for their own amusement and pleasure. That is all their life consists of. The life-giving Word, which could make a real man or woman out of them, is hitting them, but it cannot find root and grow up. There is no place left in their hearts.

Then there is what Jesus calls "desire for other things," or what we might call "restlessness." These are people who are always shifting from one thing to another. James Michener wrote a book, *The Drifters,* in which he describes this kind of people, especially young people, who cannot stay in one place long enough to put down roots but drift from one experience to another. Jesus says they are losing the truth of the delivering Word. They are choked by life.

But then there is the receptive heart, the one ready to receive —open and responsive immediately. I talked recently with a prominent businessman who told me about how he became a Christian. He had been raised with no church background at all and had four different sets of foster parents before he was eighteen. He had tried various philosophies in his search for answers to the riddle of life. Among them were transcendental meditation and Eastern religions. None of this satisfied him.

One day a friend invited him to go to church, and he went— for the first time in his life. The pastor spoke about Christ. Afterward he met the pastor and said to him, "Sir, if I understand you correctly, Christianity is saying that up here is God; down here is man; and in between is Jesus Christ; and that he is the key for man to reach God. Is that right?" The pastor said, "Yes, that's right. In fact, you've accurately described a verse in Scripture which says: 'For there is one God, and there is one mediator between God and men, the man Christ Jesus'" (1 Tim. 2:5). This man said, "Well, that makes sense to me."

Why Not Now?

The pastor responded, "I've got a book here I'd like you to take home and read. And next week, if you come back and have read it, we'll sit down and talk about it together." The man said to the pastor, "Well, I appreciate that. But tell me: If it is true that Jesus really is the way to God, then why do I have to wait till next week? Why can't I come to him now? If it really works, it will work now; if it doesn't work, it never will." The pastor said, "You're exactly right." So they bowed their heads, and the man received Christ, became a Christian immediately. He received the Word, has grown in grace ever since, and has become a strong testimony for Christ.

That is the responsive heart which is ready to act. It is true not only at the initial stages of Christianity, but whenever the Word falls on us, whenever the seed is being sown. And areas of our life are either ready to respond, or, like any of the other kinds of soil, reject the truth. This is the way the kingdom of God, the rule of God, comes into our hearts. The great question, then, is: Examine your heart when the Word is being sown. What is it like? What is it like right now?

The second parable is found in verses 26 to 29, where our Lord speaks of the seed growing secretly:

> And he said, "The kingdom of God is as if a man should scatter seed upon the ground, and should sleep and rise night and day, and the seed should sprout and grow, he knows not how. The earth produces of itself, first the blade, then the ear, then the full grain in the ear. But when the grain is ripe, at once he puts in the sickle, because the harvest has come" (Mk. 4:26–29).

This is a secret of the kingdom of God, and to me it is one of the most encouraging of all the parables Jesus ever uttered. He is speaking of how this rule of God increases, how it grows in a life. He explains it as a coming to harvest by a patient expectation that God will work. The key of this whole passage is, ". . . the seed grows, he knows not how. The earth bears fruit of itself . . ." That is, there are forces at work which will be faithful to perform their work—whether a man stews and frets about it or not. He does what he can do, what is expected of him. But then God must work. And God *will* work. And in the confidence of that, this man rests secure.

As Jesus draws the picture, this farmer goes out to sow. It is hard work as he sows the field, but this is what he can do. But then he goes home and goes to bed. He does not sit up all night biting his fingernails, wondering if the seed fell in the right places or whether it will take root. Nor does he rise the next morning and go out and dig it up to see whether or not it has sprouted yet. He rests secure in the fact that God is at work, that he has a part in this process, and he must do it; no one can do it for him. But he *will* faithfully perform it. So the farmer rests secure, knowing that as the seed grows there are stages which are observable: ". . . first the blade, then the ear, then the full grain in the ear." It is only as the grain is ripe that he is called into action again. When the harvest is ready, then he is to act once more.

This is exactly what Paul describes for us in that passage in 1 Corinthians 3:9, "For we are laborers together with God . . ." (KJV). This is the way we ought to expect him to work. It involves a witness first, perhaps a word of teaching or exhortation to someone—or to ourselves. And then an inevitable process begins, one which takes time and patience and allows God to work. One of the most destructive forces at work in the church today is our insistent demand for instant results. We want to have immediate conversions, immediate responses, and immediate dedications every time we speak. We tend not to allow time for the Word to take root and grow and come to harvest. But our Lord is teaching us the great truth that we ought to wait.

I have been watching a boy in our congregation growing up since grade school. I watched him come into adolescence and enter into a period of deep and bitter rebellion against God. I watched his parents, hurt and crushed by his attitudes, yet, nevertheless, praying for him—saying what they could to him —but above all holding him up in prayer. I watched the whole process as the seed which had been sown in his heart took root and began to grow. There were tiny observable signs of change occurring. Gradually, he came back to the Lord and opened up to the Christian family. That is the Word growing secretly. The sower knows not how it happens, but he can rest secure in this. Our Lord is teaching us the fantastic truth that God is at work. It does not all depend on us! Once we have done what has been given us to do, then we are to rest in the fact that God will work.

No Such Plant

The parable of the mustard seed is the last of this trio:

And he said, "With what can we compare the kingdom of God, or what parable shall we use for it? It is like a grain of mustard seed, which, when sown upon the ground, is the smallest of all the seeds on earth; yet when it is sown it grows up and becomes the greatest of all shrubs, and puts forth large branches, so that the birds of the air can make nests in its shade" (Mk. 4:30–32).

This is perhaps one of the most puzzling of the parables. Many have pondered long hours over it because it seems to be contrary to nature. Mustard seeds simply do not grow into great shrubs with large branches in which birds build nests. They do not grow like that here in California; they do not grow like that in Palestine. Nor have they ever done so. Any reports of "mustard trees" you may have read in reference books refer to plants which are very unlikely to be mustard.

Then what is all this about? I think we get a clue to the strange character of this parable in the way our Lord introduces it. He sounds almost puzzled: "Now, how can I illustrate this? With what can I compare the kingdom of God, or what parable shall I use?" There is an element about this which is different, unusual, and even Jesus is hard-pressed to find a natural illustration for it. Then he tells the parable of the mustard seed.

Anyone who has read the New Testament knows that Jesus frequently used the mustard seed as a symbol of faith. It is a beautiful symbol. Matthew 17:20 says, ". . . if you have faith as a grain of mustard seed, you will say to this mountain, 'Move hence to yonder place,' and it will move . . ." Our dear friend, Lillian Dickson, has an agency in Taiwan she calls "The Mustard Seed." It is an umbrella organization which sponsors many various and great works she has begun, all of which rest upon faith.

Mustard seed is an excellent symbol of faith because of two of its qualities. First, there is the quality of a seed itself—its inherent capacity for growth. A seed is able to grow, and so can faith. In fact, faith that is not used will not grow; but if it is used, it increases. This is why Jesus uses a seed as a symbol of faith. And this is why you never have to worry about whether your faith is small or great. If it is small, it can grow and eventually become large. That is where all great faith has come from—from people trusting God in little things, then in larger things, more and more, until their faith grows to take on great things. That is an invariable principle of the Word of God. When you trust him in little things, you learn to trust him in larger things; you find your faith has grown, and you are able to step out a little farther.

It is also *mustard* seed. Mustard has a particular characteristic. When I grew up as a boy in Montana, we had no doctors available, and no medicine. So whenever we got a cold, there was a single remedy: A mustard plaster was placed upon our chest—a sticky, smelly, gooey mess. It was not there very long before it began to irritate and burn and stimulate. The flesh turned red. In fact, if you did not watch it, it would actually blister the skin. I do not know how it worked, but it seemed to cure colds. But that is a quality of mustard—to irritate, to stimulate. And that is a quality of faith. If your faith is growing, someone else's is growing too. Your faith will stimulate others to have faith. Soon it spreads through the Christian body, and people begin to walk in faith who had never walked before. That, Jesus said, is what the kingdom of God is like. It has the quality of mustard seeds about it. It is to be planted so it will grow and work in this remarkable way.

But the amazing thing about this parable is that the mustard seed does not grow true to life. It acts as no other mustard seed has ever acted before. It is intended by nature to be a low shrub, no more than eight to ten feet high at best, very spindly, certainly not able to support a nest of birds. It is a rather fragile shrub, and yet pungent and powerful in its effect. That is what the church ought to be—lowly and unimpressive, and yet powerful in society. But according to Jesus, this mustard seed would grow into a great, impressive shrub, probably twenty feet high, with large branches able to support nests, and birds would come and build nests in its shade. But true mustard has never grown like that, anywhere. That would be contrary to its nature.

False Growth

Well, what does this mean? Our Lord is telling us a secret of the kingdom of God. He says that this mustard seed, which is supposed to be lowly and unimpressive, will provoke a false growth. It will stimulate a wholly false system which will be characterized by its seeking to be dominant—very impressive and powerful—and to exercise wide influence, so much so that satanic forces (you remember that in the parable of the sower, the key to all the parables, this is what Jesus says the birds represent) will take up residence within its great structure. It will seem to be tremendously powerful and have the name of the kingdom of God, but it will be anything but!

Now we know, after twenty centuries of history, that this is exactly what has happened. Great churches have grown up, seeking worldly power and influence, seeking to dominate political life and influence people in this way. This has been true not only of the Catholic church but of Protestant churches as well.

I am always amazed at the things evangelicals regard as marks of a successful church. Usually it is numbers. If you can just get a crowd of people coming, that is a successful church! And yet the cults usually can attract more people than we can. Money is another common measure; a large budget, especially a large missionary budget, is a mark of success. Or if you have impressive, beautiful buildings with costly art and expensive architecture, that is a sign of success. Or, amazingly enough, some regard the number of buses a church operates as a sign of success today! Yet we forget that in the Book of Revelation, Jesus warned the church: "For you say, I am rich, I have prospered, and I have need of nothing; not knowing that you are wretched, pitiable, poor, blind, and naked" (Rev. 3:17). None of these things are marks of success in the true church.

What is the mark of success? In Ephesians 4 Paul exhorts the church in Ephesus to "lead a life worthy of the calling to which you have been called." A worthy church, a successful church, Paul says, is one characterized by "lowliness and meekness, with patience, forbearing one another in love, eager to maintain the unity of the Spirit in the bond of peace" (Eph. 4:1–3). *That* is a successful church—where people are growing in lowliness, not seeking to lift themselves up but to be powerful where they are, with a low profile, but, nevertheless, extremely stimulating, even irritating to the community around; ". . . with patience, forbearing one another in love"—getting along together, forgiving one another, loving one another, reaching out and sharing, being open with one another. This is a successful church, ". . . eager to maintain the unity of the Spirit in the bond of peace."

There are the three secrets of the kingdom of God which Mark selects for us. What do they say to us? God is at work today just as he was then. He is sowing the Word by various means in our lives and hearts. We are to be careful that our hearts are ready and responsive to receive that Word. Then we are to rest upon him. He is bearing the load of the battle. The battle is the Lord's, not ours. He is working out his purposes in our individual lives and in the life of the church as a whole. He will do it. We can rest on it till the harvest time comes; then he will call us to action again. Finally, we are to be lowly, not seeking for status or advancement, but stimulating one another in the same way as mustard seeds. And when we do so, we can expect to provoke this whole false system which will rise on every side. But we are to walk worthy of God, in the way he has called us, eager to maintain the unity of the Spirit.

9

Why Are You Afraid?

Now we come to two incidents—the stilling of the storm on the Sea of Galilee and the healing of the demoniac—both of which deal with the problem of fear. These are fearful times, and the record of the past few years has not given us any reason to be less fearful as we face the future. It gives the heart a little clutch to think of the possibilities of what could come. The Scriptures deal often with the subject of fear because it is so common to our humanity, and these two incidents are particularly helpful. The background of the first is in chapter 4, verses 35 and 36:

On that day, when evening had come, he said to them, "Let us go across to the other side." And leaving the crowd, they took him with them, just as he was, in the boat. And other boats were with him (Mk. 4:35–36).

It is clear that this comes when our Lord was at the point of utter physical exhaustion. You remember that in this section of Mark we are dealing with a theme which Mark emphasizes in several incidents—the effects of popularity upon the ministry of Jesus. The first incidents revealed to us the satanic opposition that popularity awakened. Then in the next section we saw how this popularity necessitated a dimming of light, as manifested in the parables Jesus began to speak.

And now we come to the physical exhaustion produced by the tremendous demands of the crowds upon Jesus. Here he is, at the end of a very heavy day of teaching, of ministering, and of healing. He is worn out. He gets in the boat and says to the disciples, "Let's get away. Let's go to the other side of the lake"—to the eastern shore about five miles away. Mark makes clear that this was unpremeditated on Jesus' part: "They took him with them, just as he was." He made no preparation for this journey. And the incident which follows grew out of these circumstances.

No Hallucination

Mark also indicates that there were certain witnesses present to testify to the unusual phenomenon which occurred: "And other boats were with him." Mark adds that to reassure us that what happened during that journey was not a hallucination. One of the popular commentators on this section suggests that there really was no stilling of the storm, that what happened in the midst of this great storm was that our Lord merely settled the disciples' fear, and that there was a great calm in their hearts. It was the peace that came into their hearts which made them think he had done a miracle and stilled the storm. But this does not take note of the fact that there were other boats nearby whose occupants saw this miracle and bore witness of it. The incident is recorded in the verses that follow:

And a great storm of wind arose, and the waves beat into the boat, so that the boat was already filling. But he was in the stern, asleep on the cushion; and they woke him and said to him, "Teacher, do you not care if we perish?" And he awoke

and rebuked the wind, and said to the sea, "Peace! Be still!"
And the wind ceased and there was a great calm (Mk. 4:37–
39).

All the raw elements of drama are contained in that incident.
There is the raging storm which came suddenly upon the sea.
This happens yet today in the rugged country to the northeast
of the Sea of Galilee, what today we call the Golan Heights.
In that broken, torn terrain, it is easy for the winds to gather
and suddenly to break out upon the sea, and a violent and
raging storm can arise in just a few moments. As these
disciples set out in the calm of the evening to cross to the
eastern shore, such a storm broke out. Within moments the
sea was frothing, waves mounting up. It was a *great* wind,
Mark says. They found themselves in the midst of this tremendous, raging storm, the boat filling rapidly as water came
dashing over the bow. The disciples panicked! Sailors though
they were, they knew this storm was greater than anything
they had seen before, and they feared they were going to
perish. So they came and woke Jesus, asking, "Teacher, do
you not care that we perish?"

This indicates the storm had already begun when Jesus went
to sleep. If it had not, they would not have charged him with
indifference in their plight. If he had gone to sleep immediately
and not even known the storm had arisen, they would have
wakened him to let him know. But they charged him with indifference. In the midst of a growing peril, Jesus had gone to
sleep. This is what bothered the disciples. So they came to him,
concerned and upset not only because of their common peril
but because of the apparent indifference of the Lord to their
need.

But then as they woke him, our Lord arose and, without saying a word to them at first, rebuked the wind and, literally,
"muzzled" the sea. I do not know what they expected him to
do, but what he did do took them utterly by surprise; they did

not expect it. But they were panicky, and when we panic, this is our attitude, is it not? They were saying, in effect, "Don't just lie there; do something!" So he arose, and his first words were to rebuke the wind and muzzle the sea. He said to the wind, "Peace!" and to the sea, "Be still!" And what happened astonished these disciples—there suddenly came a great calm.

The Sudden Stillness

Now, the miracle lies not in the stilling of the storm, for even nature would do that eventually, but in the suddenness with which it happened. All of a sudden the wind, which had been roaring and beating about their ears, stopped, and there was absolute stillness. And the waves, which had been dashing over the bow, filling the boat, threatening them, mounting up higher on every side, were suddenly stilled, as though a giant hand pressed them down, and there was a great calm. This is what impressed them. All the way across the lake to the other side and to the mountains on the east, the whole lake suddenly stilled, and they realized that this was indeed a supernatural stilling of the storm.

When the account says that the Lord rebuked the wind and spoke to the sea, "Be muzzled, Be quiet!" we need to understand that he was not really speaking to the elements. After all, what good does it do to address the air as it is flowing by? Or to speak to water that is raging? I think of the story of the king who tried to stop the tides, commanding them to cease, and they ignored him, as tides will, and came rolling right on in. No, I do not think our Lord was really speaking to these elements of air and sea. What we need to understand from this is that he, knowing so clearly and so well that which is invisible to us and which we so often forget, spoke rather to the demonic forces behind the raging of the storm and the sea.

We must never forget that we live in a fallen world, and that, as the Scriptures tell us, the whole world is in the grip of the devil and his agents. This includes the physical world as well. Behind the disasters we read of so frequently and sometimes experience—earthquakes, famines, floods, droughts, cyclones, tornados, hurricanes—is often the malevolent attack of Satan upon humanity. Jesus understood this, and he rebuked not the wind but the one who aroused it. He lived in the constant realization, as the apostle Paul said, that we wrestle not against flesh and blood but against principalities and powers, wicked spirits in high places, who are able to affect humanity at various levels of life. It was these Jesus rebuked. Interestingly, the words he used here are exactly the same he used when he rebuked the demon that interrupted his discourse in the synagogue at Capernaum, as recorded in the first chapter of Mark. So he is addressing the unseen, invisible world here. The result was a great calm.

Faith Answers Fear

Then he chided the disciples: "He said to them, 'Why are you afraid?' " Is that not a strange question to ask men who were in danger of losing their lives? Just a moment earlier they were tossing about in a boat which was filling rapidly with water, in the midst of a raging storm, with no hope of help. Why shouldn't they be afraid? Yet Jesus asked them, "Why are you afraid?" And then he put his finger on the reason: "Have you no faith?"

This is why people become afraid—because they lose faith. Faith is the answer to fear. This is the first lesson which comes to us out of this incident. Faith is always the answer to our fears, regardless of what they are. Jesus put his finger right on it: "Have you no faith?"

Well, evidently they did not. They had forgotten all the things he said to them in the Sermon on the Mount about the extent of God's care for them: "You are much more valuable than flowers and birds. God cares for them; will he not much more care for you, O ye of little faith?" Here he was in the boat with them; their fate would be his fate, and yet they had forgotten this.

How would these men have acted, do you think, if they had had faith? Suppose their faith had been strong—their faith in him and in God's care and love—what would they have done? One thing is certain: they would not have wakened him; they would have let him rest. He was weary and tired and needed the rest badly. They would have done so because their faith would have reminded them of two great facts: One, the boat will not sink; it cannot sink when the Master of ocean and earth and sky is in it. Two, the storm will not last forever.

A year or so ago a good friend of mine, a handsome young evangelist from another country, told me about all the troubles he and his wife were going through. He was very dejected. She was struggling with severe physical problems—ill health arising from asthma and bronchitis which constantly kept her down. They had gone through years of struggle with this condition of hers already, and it seemed to pull the bottom out of everything he attempted to do. Here they were planning to go back to their own country, and now she was sick again.

I remember turning to this incident in Mark, reciting this story, and then saying to him, "Remember, the boat will not sink, and the storm will not last forever. That is having faith—to remember those facts." He thanked me, we prayed together and he left. I did not see him for a couple of months; then we ran into each other. I said, "How are things going? How is your wife?" He said, "Oh, not much better. She's still having terrible struggles. She can't breathe, and she can't take care of the children or the house. We're having a hard time. But I do remember two things: the boat will not sink, and the storm will not last forever!" So I prayed with him again.

Sometime later I received a note from him. They had gone back to their country, and there they had found the answer. A doctor discovered a deficiency in her diet which needed to be remedied. When that was done, the asthma and bronchitis disappeared, she was in glorious, radiant health, and they were rejoicing together. At the bottom of the page he had written, "The boat will not sink, and the storm will not last forever."

Then, very recently, I received a note that read, "This past week this young man sent word that his wife is in the hospital, and the doctors suspect leukemia. Her asthma is under control. Pray that he will remember what you told him about the boat and the storm." So a new storm has broken out in their lives. But remember, the boat will not sink, and the storm will not last forever. As C. S. Lewis wrote,

> I'll tell you how to look at it. Haven't you noticed how, in our own little war here on earth, there are different phases, and while any one phase is going on people get into the habit of thinking and behaving as if it were going to be permanent? But really the thing is changing under your hands all the time, and neither your assets nor your dangers are the same as the year before.

The significance of this event to us is that faith is the answer to fear—faith in the goodness and care of God in our lives, faith that he loves us and he is able to work in our midst. But there is still another lesson. It is that failure in faith is the doorway to greater vision. What happened here?

> He said to them, "Why are you afraid? Have you no faith?" And they were filled with awe, and said to one another, "Who then is this, that even wind and sea obey him?" (Mk. 4:40–41).

The word translated "awe" means "fear," but it is a different kind of fear than that which occurs earlier. Then it was cowardly fear; here it is that sense of deep respect which has awe at its heart. Thus, out of the failure of their faith came this deeper impression, this glimpse into the mystery of his

Personhood, which filled them with a deep sense of awe: "Who can this be, that even wind and sea obey him, who controls all the elements of the natural world. Who then is this?" The wonderful thing about this incident is that even though the disciples flunked their examination in faith, the groundwork was laid for a new expression of faith the next time they were under test. Thus, their failure opened the possibility for a new expression of faith to come.

This is the way the Lord works in our life. He does this very same thing with us. He tests our faith all the time in order that we might grow. And if our faith is strong enough, we will see that he can handle the problem, that he knows how. But even if our faith is weak, he still will not let us collapse utterly. He will hold us up and see us through and, somehow in the process, lay the foundation of a new glimpse of his might and power which will enable our faith to grow stronger for the next time.

Let us turn now to the next incident, which follows immediately in chapter 5:

They came to the other side of the sea, to the country of the Gerasenes. And when he had come out of the boat, there met him out of the tombs a man with an unclean spirit, who lived among the tombs; and no one could bind him any more, even with a chain; for he had often been bound with fetters and chains, but the chains he wrenched apart, and the fetters he broke in pieces; and no one had the strength to subdue him. Night and day among the tombs and on the mountains he was always crying out, and bruising himself with stones. And when he saw Jesus from afar, he ran and worshiped him [i.e., knelt before him]; and crying out with a loud voice, he said, "What have you to do with me, Jesus, Son of the Most High God? I adjure you by God, do not torment me." For he had said to him, "Come out of the man, you unclean spirit!" And Jesus asked him, "What is your name?" He replied, "My name is Legion; for we are many." And he begged him eagerly not to

send them out of the country [to the abyss]. Now a great herd
of swine was feeding there on the hillside; and they begged
him, "Send us to the swine, let us enter them." So he gave them
leave. And the unclean spirits came out, and entered the swine;
and the herd, numbering about two thousand, rushed down
the steep bank into the sea, and were drowned in the sea
(Mk. 5:1-13).

This incident opens before us again the whole realm of the
occult and the demonic and the oppression of mankind by
these evil and unclean spirits. In this day we have seen ample
demonstration of the actuality of these forces in our world, and
perhaps we are much more prepared to understand this story
than we would have been ten years ago. In this account we have
a very remarkable listing for us of the signs of demon possession.

I was interested to note that the New Testament never
actually uses the term "demon possession." It is a term which
has been invented, but it may not be very accurate. The word
in Scripture is always "demonized." Whether it means possession or control or influence or whatever, this is the word which
is used. We have read into it the idea of "demon possession."
Perhaps that is an accurate term; I am not prepared, at the
moment at least, to say categorically that it is not. But I do
not think it wise to use it because it is not used in Scripture.

Demons at Work

It is evident that there are various stages and degrees to
which demons, evil spirits, can affect and possess or control
human beings. In this incident we have an extreme case, and
there are listed here some seven signs which indicate when
demonic spirits are at work in the life of an individual. The
first is the world "unclean." As I mentioned earlier, there is
always an element of the unclean present in demonic effect.
In this case, the man lived among the tombs, i.e., among the

dead bodies in the limestone caves which lined the cliffs along the Sea of Galilee where they placed their dead. You always find this unclean element—the demonic living in the midst of dirt and squalor and rubbish, or evidencing moral pollution. It is no accident that the rise of satanism and occultism in these last few years has been coincidental with the spread of pornography and obscenity in the media, in our movies, and in literature. These are always related.

The second sign evident here is the isolation in which this man lived. He had a home and he had friends because Jesus sent him back to both at the end of the story. But he chose to live by himself in utter segregation, away from humanity, cut off from them. In every case of demonic influence you find this attitude of withdrawal, a desire to be separate physically or emotionally from other people.

Then there was the supernatural strength he exhibited. This is often the case. There are many instances today of people possessed or controlled by demons exercising unusual strength. This man had been bound with chains and fetters. But he had snapped the chains and torn off the fetters and no one had the strength to subdue him—a remarkable demonstration of demonic power.

Another mark which is always present is a sense of torment. This man was tormented. At first, demonic influence can seem to be very alluring and seductive, very attractive and fascinating. But that is designed to lead one on until finally this torment sets in, the deep sense of restlessness which this man exhibited, wandering up and down the mountains, crying out in pain at the torment he felt within, bruising himself with stones— evidently in an attempt to drive out his inner torment. This is very characteristic of demonic influence.

Another element always present is the immediate recognition of the authority of Jesus. This man, when he saw Jesus, knew immediately who he was. He came running to him and called him by name, using the phrase demons always employ, "Son of the Most High God." This is very revealing because it is the highest name a nonbeliever can know or use to refer to God— "the Most High God." It is used all through the Old Testament by members of the gentile nations. Israel knew him as "Jehovah"—"Lord"; everyone else knew him as "El Elyon"— "God Most High." This is how the demons refer to him.

Then there is the duality or multiplicity of personality which is exhibited here. Notice verse 9: "Jesus asked him, 'What is your name?' He replied, 'My name is Legion, for *we* are many.' " And in verse 10 the demoniac begged Jesus not to send *them* to the abyss. There is this awareness of at least a double personality.

The last mark is that of suicidal tendencies, the destructiveness which is present in demonic influence. Not all suicidal tendencies come from demonic influence, but this is clearly a mark here. When the demons were cast out, they entered into the swine, and what did they do? All two thousand of them rushed down the mountainside and drowned in the sea. Thus the demons, who had asked to enter the swine in order not to go into the abyss, defeated their own purpose and, because of the death of the swine, had to enter the abyss anyway. That is why Jesus gave them permission to enter into the swine. The death of the swine was a tremendous testimony to this man that he was indeed free from the demons that had inhabited him. But it was also the means by which these demons were sent into the abyss where they belonged.

Not So Strange Reaction

Now we have the sequel to the story:

The herdsmen fled, and told it in the city and in the country. And people came to see what it was that had happened. And they came to Jesus, and saw the demoniac sitting there, clothed and in his right mind, the man who had had the legion; and they were afraid. And those who had seen it told what had happened to the demoniac and to the swine. And they began to beg Jesus to depart from their neighborhood (Mk. 5:14–17).

What a strange reaction—and yet it is not so strange, is it? When these people heard the news several hours later, they came to see what had happened. By this time the man had gone home and clothed himself, had come back to Jesus, and was sitting at his feet, listening to him. They saw him sitting there at rest—this man who had been so restless—and clothed, prepared to enter society again, no longer withdrawn, afraid of people. And he was in his right mind—at peace with himself, no civil war raging within any longer. They saw this deliverance. It was evident to them that here was a man set free.

But they are hit in the tenderest part of their anatomy—their pocketbook. And instead of rejoicing, they plead with Jesus to leave. Society is always doing this. Whenever there is a question of the welfare of an individual versus the wealth of the many, society invariably chooses the wealth of the many rather than the welfare of one. Twenty-five years or more ago, I read a poem by John Oxenham based upon this incident in Scripture. I never memorized it all, but one stanza sticks in my memory. He put it very graphically. These people came to Jesus and said to him, "Rabbi, be gone! And take this fool of thine! You love his soul; we prefer swine."

Well, the end of the story is that as Jesus, obeying this injunction to leave the neighborhood,

. . . was getting into the boat, the man who had been possessed with demons begged him that he might be with him. But he refused, and said to him, "Go home to your friends, and tell them how much the Lord has done for you, and how he has had mercy on you." And he went away and began to proclaim in the Decapolis how much Jesus had done for him; and all men marveled (Mk. 5:18–20).

The Decapolis was ten Greek cities on the eastern side of the sea of Galilee, including Damascus. It was to this gentile community that Jesus commanded this man to go and bear witness. Among the Jews, he told them not to say a word, lest he be overwhelmed by people mobbing him, making impossible an orderly ministry. But here among the gentiles he sent this man back. What a beautiful pattern of witness he established! He told him to go home, and not to go around from door to door explaining the plan of salvation, but simply to tell his friends what happened to him. That is what a witness is. I am not against evangelizing, but we need to understand that witnessing and evangelizing are two different things. This man was sent to be a witness, to tell people what had happened to him. And what a story he had to tell—of how he had lived in anguish and torment, how he had been against all of humanity, a menace to anyone who came by, angry and hostile and rebellious; and yet Jesus had freed him, given him peace and joy! No wonder that as he went about in all these cities, men marveled at what they heard.

Now what is the significance of these two incidents in our lives? Mark has put them together to help us to see that Jesus is Lord—whether the enemy that threatens us and frightens us in some circumstance or event outside us, as the storm was for the disciples, or whether that which betrays and subverts us and sabotages everything we try to do is something arising from within—some habit, some attitude, some long-standing hostility or resentment we bear against another, or even some demonic influence which is ripping and tearing us apart, making us restless and discontent. Whatever it is, Jesus is Lord. This is the message of these stories. Within or without, he reigns now in our lives. Therefore, his question to us always is, "Why are you afraid? Have you no faith?"

10

The Weakness of the World

Three incidents in the life of the Servant of God—the intermingled incidents of the raising from the dead of the daughter of Jairus and the healing of the woman with the issue of blood, and then the second visit of our Lord to his hometown of Nazareth—close a section in the Gospel of Mark whose theme is the effects of popularity. These incidents illustrate the impotence of nature, the weakness of the world, the inability of natural life to supply the needs of suffering hearts. We have two sufferers in this first account: Jairus, the ruler of the synagogue, whose problem was fear and sorrow at the death of his daughter; and the woman who for twelve years endured the pain and shame and heartache of an issue of blood. We look first at the coming of Jairus, beginning with verse 21:

And when Jesus had crossed again in the boat to the other side, a great crowd gathered about him; and he was beside the sea. Then came one of the rulers of the synagogue, Jairus by name; and seeing him, he fell at his feet, and besought him, saying, "My little daughter is at the point of death. Come and lay your hands on her, so that she may be made well, and live." And he went with him. And a great crowd followed him and thronged about him (Mk. 5:21–24).

It must have been very difficult for Jairus to come to Jesus. Mark tells us that Jairus was one of the rulers of the synagogue, and at this time the synagogues were practically closed to the ministry of Jesus. He had healed so many people on the sabbath day and had offended the Pharisees so much that they had cut him off from this ministry within the synagogue. Now he was out in the open countryside, preaching on the hillsides. Yet here is one of the rulers, the chief man of the most prominent synagogue of Capernaum—what would correspond to the "Chairman of the Board of Elders" of that synagogue— who comes to Jesus and beseeches him to heal his daughter. I am sure he had to overcome problems of pride, prejudice, and even of shame and embarrassment before he could come to this itinerant teacher who had been rejected by the leading scholars and teachers of that day, this "tub-thumping rabble-rouser" who went around from village to village teaching things which were upsetting the people and, in the eyes of the Pharisees at least, often contrary to the law of Moses. Now Jairus had to leave his privileged position and come and fall at Jesus' feet and beseech him for help.

A Desperate Father

But although there were certain forces which hindered his coming, there was also an overriding fear which drove him to Jesus—the fact that his twelve-year-old little girl lay sick, almost ready to die, and he knew it. Here was a desperate father. Those of you who are parents know that there is no agony like that you feel when your little one is threatened with death. If you have ever stood by a crib, as I have, watching a little head tossing in a high fever, you know something of the terrible clutch of fear which comes to your heart in those moments.

I will never forget the time a number of years ago when my wife and I were driving through Oregon with our little daughter, Susan. She had developed a fever the night before, when we were staying in a motel, but it didn't seem serious. As we drove along, all of a sudden, as she lay in her mother's arms, she went into convulsions. Her eyes turned up, her body began to jerk, and she obviously was in great danger. I remember how my heart clutched. I stopped the car, grabbed her, stumbled across the road to a farmhouse. It was about six o'clock in the morning, but I thundered on the door. A lady came to the door, and I said, "My daughter is very sick—she's in convulsions. Do you have a bathtub where we can put her in warm water?" The lady was so taken aback she hardly knew what to say. She motioned down the hall, and without waiting for any word I pushed the door open, went down the hall, and started running water in the tub. We found out later that this family had the only bathtub and the only phone in that area for miles around. We called a doctor and arranged to take the baby to him. It turned out all right, but I have never forgotten that moment when it looked as though she were going to die. This is what drove Jairus, this agonized father, to Jesus—the fear that this little one, who had blessed their home and filled it with sunshine for twelve years, was to be taken from them.

But there is also evidence of the faith which drew him. Mark is careful to tell us that when he came he fell down at Jesus' feet and said, "My daughter is at the point of death. Come and lay your hands on her, so that she may be made well, and live." This man, prominent though he was, nevertheless knew that there was power in Jesus, and it was that which drew him. He forgot his pride and his prejudice, and he came and asked for help.

At this point Mark leaves the story and turns to the interruption which came as Jesus and Jairus were on their way to the house together. Our Lord responded instantly to this man's agony and went with him. On the way, Mark tells us, they

met a woman who had had a flow of blood for twelve years.
(There is an interesting emphasis on the number twelve here;
the little girl was twelve years old and the woman had a flow
of blood for twelve years.)

> And there was a woman who had had a flow of blood for
> twelve years, and who had suffered much under many physicians,
> and had spent all that she had, and was no better but rather
> grew worse (Mk. 5:25–26).

Mark is careful to tell us three things about this woman:
her condition, her cure, and her confession before Jesus. Look
at her condition. She was suffering from what doctors would
call a vaginal hemorrhage, a continual flow of blood which not
only gave her great distress and pain but also rendered her
ceremonially unclean so that she was ostracized by society.
She had to keep her distance from everyone; she could not
mingle with people. She was almost like a leper. People were
forbidden to touch her while she was in this condition. She was
forbidden to attend services in the temple or in the synagogue.
So for twelve years she had been denied all the comfort and
solace of the services of the people of God. She was ostracized,
separated, isolated, and in pain and distress from this unending
flow of blood.

To make matters even worse, she had spent all her money
on doctors and had not been helped a bit. Some of us can
sympathize. Many doctors are dedicated, marvelous men who
have done great work. But there are times when doctors fail,
and this was such a time. Mark seems to imply that none of
them had the grace to tell her they could not help her; they
simply took her money, but left her unchanged.

The Touch of Faith

When she came to Jesus, something wonderful happened:

She had heard the reports about Jesus, and came up behind him in the crowd and touched his garment. For she said, "If I touch even his garments, I shall be made well." And immediately the hemorrhage ceased; and she felt in her body that she was healed of her disease (Mk. 5:27–29).

We do not know how she had heard of Jesus, but the reports had come to her and her hopes had been awakened. Here was One who, after these long years, might be able to do something about her tragic condition. And when her hopes were awakened, her faith was aroused, and she became convinced that Jesus could indeed help her. But she had a problem because she could not come like anyone else and talk to him. She was unclean, and it was forbidden for her to get close to anyone or to talk to them. She knew she could not come by the usual route. But her faith was aroused to the point that she said, "If I can just touch him—just touch his garments—I'll be made well." So, when she saw the crowd pressing all around him, she was determined to get through. In desperation she pushed her way through the crowd, ignoring the fact that she was rendering others unclean by that action. Finally, she had wormed her way through until she could touch the hem of his garment. The moment she laid hold of it, she felt the issue of blood stop, and she knew that she was healed.

There is a wonderful picture here, in that this woman, with a touch of faith, draws power from Jesus, whereas all the rest of the crowd, pressing around him on every side, touching him many times in the course of the journey, were not receiving anything from him. In fact, the disciples commented on this, as Mark goes on to tell us:

And Jesus, perceiving in himself that power had gone forth from him, immediately turned about in the crowd, and said, "Who touched my garments?" And his disciples said to him, "You see the crowd pressing around you, and yet you say, 'Who touched

me?' " And he looked around to see who had done it. But the
woman, knowing what had been done to her, came in fear and
trembling and fell down before him, and told him the whole
truth. And he said to her, "Daughter, your faith has made you
well; go in peace, and be healed of your disease" (Mk. 5:30–
34).

The fact that the Lord knew something had happened to him
when she touched him is in some measure indicative of the
cost of his ministry. He felt power go forth from him; he felt
weaker. He was noticeably exhausted by this occurrence—to
some degree, at least. This is the first clue we have had so far
in the Gospels as to what it cost Jesus to heal people and to
minister to them as he so frequently did. No wonder he was so
physically exhausted at the end of the day! It cost him something. Power was going from him; it was a demanding ministry.

I would not want to compare this directly with the ministry
of preaching, but I know there is some similarity. An hour of
preaching is very demanding. I used to know a dear old Bible
teacher, Dr. Walter Wilson, of Kansas City. He was a medical
doctor, and then he became an outstanding Bible teacher. He
died just a couple of years ago, in his nineties. The last time I
saw him, Dr. Wilson told me how he had witnessed to Buffalo
Bill and had led Buffalo Bill's wife to the Lord. I do not know
how he arrived at his figures, but as a medical doctor he had
calculated that an hour of preaching is equal in stress and
demand to working hard at physical labor for half a day, or
working as an executive in an office for a full day. Something
of that demand is what Jesus felt here. He felt power go out
from him, he felt weaker, indicating something of the cost of
his ministry.

The Father's Work

This incident indicates, too, that the healing was really not
done by Jesus; it was done by his Father. Our Lord did not

even know it was happening. It was not his willful choice that this woman be healed. She touched him, and the touch of faith drew from him the power to heal. But he did not even know it until it happened. This is confirmation of what Jesus himself tells us—that it was not he who did the healing or the speaking; it was the Father who dwelt in him. An all-seeing God watched this woman push her way through the crowd, saw the faith in her heart. And when, in the midst of that crowd pressing all around Jesus and touching him in a dozen different ways, he saw *this* woman reach out and touch his garment, instantly the power of God flowed through the life of Jesus and healed her. This is what Jesus said: "It is not I who do the works, but the Father who dwells in me."

Yet, having said that, it is clear that our Lord did have some part in this, because when the woman, knowing that he was looking for her, fell down and told the whole truth, he said to her, "Daughter, your faith has made you well; go [literally] *into* peace, and be healed of your disease." Why would he tell her to be healed when she had already been healed? The idea expressed by the verb tense he used is, "Be continually healed." That is, he was granting her continuance in health.

This is the only time recorded in the Scriptures that he ever used this term "daughter." He was very tender with this woman because, despite her shame and embarrassment, she had blurted out the whole truth in front of the crowd. I think that is the ground upon which Jesus continued this healing, made it permanent. She told him the truth when it was embarrassing to do so. When he looked around for someone, she fell down before him and told him what her problem was, how long she had had it, how unclean she was, how difficult it was to find access to him, how determined she was. She simply put the problem right back into his hands. And immediately his response was to make permanent her healed condition. I believe that if she had not responded in that way, if she had tried to lose herself in the crowd and seek anonymity, she would have had that disease back within hours. This may explain why there are failures of some modern purported "healings."

At this point we return to the story of Jairus and his daughter. Mark tells us,

> While he was still speaking [speaking to the woman], there came from the ruler's house some who said, "Your daughter is dead. Why trouble the Teacher any further?" But ignoring what they said, Jesus said to the ruler of the synagogue, "Do not fear, only believe." And he allowed no one to follow him except Peter and James and John the brother of James. When they came to the house of the ruler of the synagogue, he saw a tumult, and people weeping and wailing loudly. And when he had entered, he said to them, "Why do you make a tumult and weep? The child is not dead but sleeping." And they laughed at him (Mk. 5:35–40).

This whole account, to this point, is designed by Mark to stress the finality of death. Here you see that awful moment when death takes over and human efforts end. Perhaps you have been involved when someone has been seized with a heart attack, or has almost drowned, and emergency efforts are being made to revive him. The paramedic squad is there. Somebody is attempting resuscitation. Everybody gathers around, tense and excited. Everyone is concentrating on the effort to revive and restore this person. Then the moment arrives when the doctor says, "He's gone." And everybody stops; all efforts to revive the person cease. They give up because death has set in. Many of you have felt that sense of finality when you have had to close the coffin on a loved one, walk away, and begin a new life. This is what Jairus felt at this moment.

Can you imagine his impatience, as he is waiting through this encounter with the woman? He stands first on one leg and then the other, waiting for Jesus to get on with it, to get to the house where his daughter is waiting. Yet he is fearful to interrupt Jesus in this obviously needy situation. Finally, just as they are ready to move on, the word comes, "Your daughter is dead," and his heart sinks.

As they come to the house the mourners have already begun their wailing cry. It was customary in those days to hire mourners to bemoan the death of an individual. There was a terrible frenzy about it. They would actually rip their garments apart, tear out their hair, and cry out with loud shrieks and howls. But even though there was some degree of professionalism about this, it represents the terrible sense of despair which people—even in Israel—had come to in the face of death. There is none of the stoic's resignation here, such as you would have seen among the Greeks, but this horrible crying out, this frenzy of despair, this sense of hopelessness at the finality of death's cold grip.

Only Believe

But in contrast to that, look at the conduct of Jesus as he meets their cynical laughter and as he acts throughout this account. First, he reassures Jairus at the moment the message reaches him. "Don't be afraid," he says "only believe." Once again we see that fear is to be met by faith. Faith is the answer to fear—believing that God knows what he is doing. This is always the answer to fear. "Only believe." Then he carefully selects Peter and James and John, and orders them to come with him, because he wants them to see something they will never forget.

And from this moment on, as we will see, Peter's account of this episode is woven through Mark's record. Even the very language Jesus used at the bedside of the little girl is repeated, for Peter never forgot it. Mark does not even put it in Greek, but leaves it in the Aramaic—the very words Jesus spoke as Peter related them to him. He records the incident which comes after her resurrection. Jesus said to the people, "Give her something to eat." Peter was amazed at this—that the Lord

Jesus would think so tenderly of her as to remember her need
for food after such an ordeal.

As they come to the house, Jesus says to the people in their
crying, frenzied activity, "Why are you carrying on like this?
She's not dead; she's asleep." We almost feel like joining them
as they laugh at him. They thought he was crazy. And yet, who
has the truer view of death, Jesus or man? Remember that
he said the same thing when he was told of Lazarus: "He is
sleeping." Again and again he refers to death as a sleep when
it involves a believer. Death is not what it appears to us when
belief and faith are present. It is merely temporary. It is nothing
more serious, as far as the believer is concerned, than going to
sleep. What a comfort those words have been to so many who
have come themselves to the edge of death and have realized
that all they were doing was really going to sleep, as Jesus has
said. Mark continues the account:

> But he put them all outside, and took the child's father and
> mother and those who were with him, and went in where the
> child was. Taking her by the hand he said to her, "Talitha
> cumi"; which means, "Little girl, I say to you, arise." And im-
> mediately the girl got up and walked; for she was twelve years
> old. And immediately they were overcome with amazement
> (Mk. 5:40–42).

Jesus puts out all the people except the father and mother
and Peter and James and John, and together they go in to the
quiet and still corpse. This father and mother are broken-
hearted, but Jesus walks to the side of the little girl and, taking
her by the hand, says in Aramaic, "Talitha cumi," which means,
literally, "Little lamb, arise." And somewhere, wherever that
spirit had gone, it heard those words of Jesus and came back
into that body, which began to flush with health and strength
and life again. He raised her up, and she walked around the
room to the amazement of all who were there.

Not for Her Sake

Now, why did Jesus do that? Well, it was not for the little girl's sake. He called her back to pain, heartache, worry, weariness, and ultimate death once again. He did it for the sake of the father and mother, to assuage their agony of heart. He responded to their sorrow and restored this little girl. "Well," you say, "that's fine. I read this story of how he healed the woman and raised the little girl. But he didn't do that for me. I'm sick, and he hasn't healed me. My loved ones are in the grave, though I wanted them back, too. Why doesn't he respond like that today?" What is the answer to that? It is evident from this account that Jesus did not heal the woman, and he did not raise the child, in order to encourage us to expect the same thing today. This is why he strictly charged that no one should know this, as Mark tells us: "And he strictly charged them that no one should know this, and told them to give her something to eat" (Mk. 5:43).

Jesus did not want this broadcast all around, so that he would get an invitation to every funeral held in Palestine for the next five years! No, he wanted us to learn something else from this. He healed this woman and raised this child in order that we might have a new view of sickness and death, a view that the world will never share, a view that will keep us steady in the midst of this kind of weakness and pressure and will hold us peaceful and calm in these terrible hours.

I want to illustrate this with a quote from Dr. G. Campbell Morgan, the great English expositor of Scripture. Perhaps you have read some of his work. His ministry has meant a great deal to me and has taught me much about expounding the Scriptures, though I never met him. There was a time when his first-born daughter lay at the point of death. Years later, speaking on this incident of the raising of Jairus' daughter, he said these words:

I can hardly speak of this matter without becoming personal and reminiscent, remembering a time forty years ago when my own first lassie lay at the point of death, dying. I called for Him then, and He came, and surely said to our troubled hearts, "Fear not, believe only." He did not say, "She shall be made whole." She was not made whole, on the earthly plane; she passed away into the life beyond. But He did say to her, "Talitha cumi," i.e., "Little lamb, arise." But in her case that did not mean, "Stay on the earth level"; it meant that He needed her, and He took her to be with Himself. She has been with Him for all these years, as we measure time here, and I have missed her every day. But His word, "Believe only," has been the strength of all the passing years.

This is what Jesus intends for us to learn from this account—that he is able to meet the suffering of the heart, whatever its cause, when the world's resources are brought to an end. All this is highlighted for us in the brief account we have next, in the opening words of chapter 6:

He went away from there and came to his own country; and his disciples followed him. And on the sabbath he began to teach in the synagogue; and many who heard him were astonished, saying, "Where did this man get all this? What is the wisdom given to him? What mighty works are wrought by his hands! Is not this the carpenter, the son of Mary and brother of James and Joses and Judas and Simon, and are not his sisters here with us?" And they took offense at him. And Jesus said to them, "A prophet is not without honor, except in his own country, and among his own kin, and in his own house." And he could do no mighty work there, except that he laid his hands upon a few sick people and healed them. And he marveled because of their unbelief. And he went about among the villages teaching (Mk. 6:1–6).

We can gather up the meaning of this whole account in just a few words: limited views mean limited lives. If your view of life is so narrow and crabbed, so withered and shrunken, as to include nothing but what you can see and feel and taste and smell and hear and reason, then your life is going to be horribly deprived and poverty-stricken. This is how it was in Nazareth. Jesus had been in Nazareth the year before. They tried to kill him on that occasion because he would not do what they wanted. Now he comes back again and teaches in the synagogue, and they are astonished. They ask the right questions: "Where did this man get all this? What is the wisdom given to him? What mighty works are wrought by his hands!" For reports had come to them.

Refuge in Ridicule

But their answers to their own questions are horribly limited. "Who is this? Is this not the carpenter? Why, he made the table in our house. I remember when we used to feed him tea and sandwiches for lunch when he came to help us build the house where I live! He was just a carpenter! And his brothers and sisters live here—we know the whole family! Why, he couldn't be this powerful a man!" And they did the incredible—they took refuge in that final resort of all weak and small minds—they ridiculed him. They took offense at him and began to discount all he had done and said: "He can't be anything, because we know him. We know his beginnings, his family, where he came from."

Jesus pointed out to them that this is characteristic of fallen human nature. There was no recognition of his worth, no honor accorded him in his own hometown. And as a result, there was no mighty work done there. He responded to the few who had faith, but there was nothing the town could boast of. And is it not amazing that through all these centuries, though Nazareth has never been forgotten as the town in which Jesus grew up, yet to this very day it is regarded in Palestine with some sense of embarrassment. Nothing honorable has ever been associated with Nazareth other than the fact that Jesus grew up there. They missed their great opportunity.

What is all this saying—this entire account of the healing of the woman, the raising of Jairus' daughter, and the reception given him by the people of Nazareth? It is saying to us today, "Lift up your eyes and look beyond the visible to the realities of God. Live in the full dimensions of life as God intended life to be." Life can never be explained entirely in terms of the natural. Its resources come to an end. Its ability to help us soon disappears. We are left impoverished and despairing if all we have to depend on are natural resources, natural power. But God is rich in grace, rich in power, rich in inward strength and sympathy, and his cry to us is, "No longer be unbelieving, but believe and have faith that I am at work, and I will enrich your life beyond your wildest dreams." As time goes on, in his own way, according to his own schedule, and through the processes of pain and toil and trouble, God will bring a depth of enrichment to you that you cannot possibly measure.

11

Who Is This?

We come now to the last section of the first half of Mark's Gospel. The theme of this section is given to us in the words of the disciples when Jesus stilled the storm on the Sea of Galilee. As he rose from sleep and commanded the wind and waves to cease and the storm subsided and there came a great calm, the disciples said in amazement to themselves, "Who then is this?" A little later when Jesus went to Nazareth, the people among whom he had grown up and whom he had served as a carpenter until he was thirty years of age said something similar when they heard him teach: "Where did he get all this?" It is striking that the unbelieving citizens of Nazareth, and these believing disciples who had accompanied Jesus for almost a year of ministry, asked the same question about him: "Who is this?"

Our Lord seems to feel it is now necessary for the disciples to begin to answer this question. So throughout this section he engages in a deliberate campaign to teach them who he is, and when we come to the end of the section, they will have arrived at the answer to this question. We begin at chapter 6, verse 7, with the sending out of the twelve disciples on a special mission:

> And he called to him the twelve, and began to send them out two by two, and gave them authority over the unclean spirits. He charged them to take nothing for their journey except a staff; no bread, no bag, no money in their belts; but to wear sandals and not put on two tunics. And he said to them, "Where you enter a house, stay there until you leave the place. And if any place will not receive you and they refuse to hear you, when you leave, shake off the dust that is on your feet for a testimony against them." So they went out and preached that men should repent. And they cast out many demons, and anointed with oil many that were sick and healed them (Mk. 6:7–13).

This ministry of the twelve disciples supplies us with a number of principles of Christian ministry. Certain aspects of their ministry were governed and controlled by the local situation, as we will see. If you want a more detailed account, you can read it in Matthew's Gospel. But in this brief survey Mark highlights three important facts.

First, he emphasizes the power these disciples exercised. Jesus sent them out, and he gave them authority over all unclean spirits. I do not know how he did this, but it is evident that our Lord was able to impart to them power which he himself possessed and which they were able to exercise at a distance from him. Much later, in the Upper Room, as he is about to leave them he says, "Another Comforter, another Strengthener, will come." This implies, of course, that one was already there—it was he. He himself supplied the power and authority they needed for this ministry.

. . . In the N–N–Name of Jesus!

I love to think these things through in my imagination, and I hope you do too when you study your Bible. I can imagine with what uncertainty these disciples must have tried this out.

There must have come a time when each one of them was confronted with a demon-possessed individual, and frightened and uncertain, they commanded the demon to depart in the name of Jesus. What a relief it must have been to see that the demons obeyed them! For when they came back, Matthew tells us, they were rejoicing that the demons were subject to them. Now, this was done in the name of Jesus; they did not go out on their own; they did not magnify themselves. They went in the name of Jesus, and in that name they had power over all the evil spirits.

Second, Mark brings out the fact that this power was expressed in unity. They did not go out all by themselves; our Lord sent them out two by two. Matthew gives us the list of who went with whom. Andrew went with Peter, his brother. James went with John, his brother. And so on down through the list. (I have always felt sorry for Simon the Zealot because his partner was Judas Iscariot! Yet is it not amazing that when these twelve were sent out, even Judas was given power to cast out demons in the name of Jesus and to heal the sick? In fact, in Matthew's account, Jesus even told them to go out and raise the dead. They were empowered to do all these mighty works in his name. This ought to give us pause when we see power and influence being exercised in the name of Jesus by people today. It does not in any way guarantee that they are genuine disciples, for here was an unbeliever, one whom Jesus called a "devil from the beginning," whom he knew from the very beginning to be just that, but who nevertheless exercised a ministry of great power along with these other disciples.) They went out two by two, in the unity of fellowship together, and this power was expressed through them.

The third fact to note is that they were given a superiority over all forms of evil. They did not need to fear anything they came up against. He gave them authority over *all* unclean spirits. This suggests to me that those of us who still go out to minister in the name of Jesus are to recognize that authority is given to us, and that we do not need to be afraid to tackle anything. There is no entrenchment of evil which is too difficult for Christians to take on. That is what this account suggests, and what these disciples discovered when they went out.

Notice the dependence they practiced, as well. Jesus made it clear they were to go without any provision for their journey. He said, in effect, "Now, don't even go home and get ready; go just as you are. Don't think about any preparations. Take no food, take no money to buy food—not even some hidden provision for emergencies in the secret compartment of your wallet. Just go trusting God all the way, and God will make provision for you." He deliberately sent them out in this way to teach them lessons in faith, to teach them that God was able to provide, that everywhere they went they would find provision made.

A Question of Dependence

We also need to recognize, however, that this was in line with the general practice of that time. That is, hospitality was considered very important in these Eastern villages. Any stranger coming to town could expect to be taken care of and entertained. So when they went, Jesus told them to expect hospitality. They did not have motels and hotels, and inns were very few, so this was the normal provision for travelers in that day. We must read this account in conjunction with Luke 22 where, much later, as Jesus came to the close of his ministry, he said to his disciples,

> "When I sent you out with no purse or bag or sandals, did you lack anything?" They said, "Nothing." He said to them, "But now, let him who has a purse take it, and likewise a bag. And let him who has no sword sell his mantle and buy one" (Luke 22:35–36).

This was to be the continuing practice in the ministry of believers, as our Lord was approaching the close of his ministry and the age of the Spirit was about to begin. I say this because there are some who, having read this account of the first mission of the twelve, immediately leap to the conclusion that their practice is to apply as much to us today, and they rush forth to minister without making any adequate preparation whatever. This shows how carelessly we sometimes read our Scripture. Our Lord makes clear that this was a temporary provision, specifically for these men. There is, however, an abiding principle which runs through all the ages and which grows out of this account: Those who go and minister in the name of Jesus, go in dependence upon God. God must open doors. God must plan the journey and make the opportunity and supply the needs, whatever the preparation made in advance. It is God upon whom we must depend. This is what our Lord was teaching these disciples.

Note, too, that they were not to go out as beggars. They were not to solicit hospitality and funds. They were going to *give,* not to *get.* They were clothed with authority, with power to bless and strengthen and heal, and they were to share their power and their peace whenever they came into a house. In the fuller account in Matthew, whenever they came to a house, they were commanded to let their peace come upon that household and were to be a blessing to the family where they stayed. Furthermore, they were to exercise the power of their ministry in that household, to heal the sick and to leave blessing behind. So, as they went, they were giving far more than they got. This, again, is an abiding principle of ministry. Ministry which is worthy of support is ministry that gives more than it gets.

Our Lord instructed them that when they left a village or a town which did not receive them, they were to leave without regret, except to express a word of sorrow. This is the meaning

of the shaking off of dust from their feet. It was not an act of
vindictiveness; it was not anger or resentment which was being
expressed. It was an attitude of sorrow that these people would
not receive the blessing which was available to them.

Notice, further, the message they preached. They went out
preaching that men should repent, the same message that was
preached by John the Baptist. Repentance is coming to the
place where you simply admit that you need help. When people
reached that place as a result of the preaching of the twelve,
then the disciples ministered to them in the unique way recorded here: "They cast out many demons, and anointed with
oil many that were sick and healed them."

Oil of Forgiveness

I confess that for years I have read this account in the
Gospels, and it never struck me that the disciples went about
anointing with oil. I never saw that until I read it again in
preparation for this study. Jesus never anointed with oil, but the
disciples did, evidently at his command. This links with a passage in James 5. James was the brother of Jesus, who grew up
with him in that home in Nazareth. He says,

> Is any among you sick? Let him call for the elders of the church,
> and let them pray over him, anointing him with oil in the name
> of the Lord; and the prayer of faith will save the sick man,
> and the Lord will raise him up; and if he has committed sins,
> he will be forgiven (James 5:14–15).

This is evidently a reference to the apostles' practice of
anointing with oil as they went about ministering from place to
place. So, as men and women came to the place of repentance,
acknowledging their guilt, their need, their wrongdoing, their
hurtful ways, then these disciples were empowered to administer
forgiveness and healing in the name of Jesus. People were to
be forgiven and raised up, when they came to the place of

repentance. This casts a great deal of light on that passage in James. The disciples' ministry was a response to the problem of sin and evil in individuals. And so we are likewise sent out, by the same Lord, with authority to act against evil wherever we find it—but in dependence upon God to open the doors and make the ways and provide the opportunities and plan the strategies. We are to declare the message that people, when they come to the place of acknowledging their need, to the place of repentance, are open to the ministry and the grace of God. What a ministry this was for the disciples, as they went about! It had a great effect.

In fact, Mark goes on to tell us what the effect was, as he links it with the event which comes before us next—the murder of John the Baptist. The account opens in verse 14 by citing the effect of the ministry of the twelve disciples:

> King Herod heard of it [their ministry]; for Jesus' name had become known. Some said, "John the baptizer has been raised from the dead; that is why these powers are at work in him." But others said, "It is Elijah." And others said, "It is a prophet, like one of the prophets of old." But when Herod heard of it he said, "John, whom I beheaded, has been raised" (Mk. 6:14–16).

Two things mark the success of the ministry of these twelve disciples as they went about from place to place. First, the name of Jesus was magnified. This indicates how faithful these men were to their commission. They did not magnify them-selves. Nowhere did people raise the question, "Who are these men that they do these mighty things?" The question raised was always, "Who is this Jesus by whose name these men are acting?" So the name of Jesus was spread abroad throughout that region. I like that. It indicates that these disciples were not keeping statistics. They did not come back with a long list of how many demons were cast out, how many people were baptized, and how many were healed, although that is the way

we might have done it. They were content to know that the
name of Jesus was magnified. Everywhere people were talking
about Jesus and what he could do. One of the great weaknesses
of the modern church is that we talk so much about the church,
instead of about the Lord and what the Lord can do.

The second result is that Herod was frightened out of his
wits. When he heard all these reports, he suddenly realized
that the fire he thought he had put out by putting John the
Baptist to death had suddenly broken out in a dozen new
places. And that scared him. This is the way God always works.
When someone raises opposition to the gospel message and
squelches it in one place, this serves only to scatter it, like pouring water on burning oil. When Herod realized this he was
very frightened.

No Miracles

It is especially remarkable that Herod actually thought this
was John the Baptist raised from the dead and appearing in all
these various places, because the Scriptures tell us specifically
that John the Baptist did no miracles! Yet when Herod hears
of all these miracles he says, "This is John, come back from the
dead." This is all the more amazing in that Herod belonged
to the party of the Sadducees, who were rationalists, anti-
supernaturalists. They did not believe in resurrection. Yet the
minute word got back to Herod that the twelve were preaching
like this, he said, "Oh, oh, it's John, raised again from the dead."
All of which testifies to the power of a guilty conscience at work
in this man. Shakespeare said, "Conscience doth make cowards
of us all." Herod is a very vivid example of that truth.

The account which follows is a flashback to an event which
happened just before the disciples were sent out:

For Herod had sent and seized John, and bound him in prison
for the sake of Herodias, his brother Philip's wife; because he

had married her. For John said to Herod, "It is not lawful for you to have your brother's wife" (Mk. 6:17–18).

The marital entanglements of this whole family of Herods are incredible. They started with Herod the Great, who married five different wives and had children by all of them. Then the progeny began to marry each other and each other's progeny! So there were cousins marrying, and, in the case of this Herod, Herod Antipas—he married his niece, Herodias, who had been the wife of his half-brother, Philip. Now, to further complicate the story, there was another half-brother also named Philip! But I am not going to try to sort it all out for you; it is enough to recognize that this was a public scandal of that day. And John the Baptist evidently had publicly rebuked the king for seducing his brother's wife and marrying her. Herod did not seem to be greatly offended by John's rebuke, but Herodias was. She insisted on John's arrest and, later, his murder.

And Herodias had a grudge against him, and wanted to kill him. But she could not, for Herod feared John, knowing that he was a righteous and holy man, and kept him safe. When he heard him, he was much perplexed: and yet he heard him gladly. But an opportunity came when Herod on his birthday gave a banquet for his courtiers and officers and the leading men of Galilee. For when Herodias' daughter [Salome] came in and danced, she pleased Herod and his guests; and the king said to the girl, "Ask me for whatever you wish, and I will grant it." And he vowed to her, "Whatever you ask me, I will give you, even half of my kingdom." And she went out, and said to her mother, "What shall I ask?" And she said, "The head of John the baptizer." And she came in immediately with haste to the king, and asked, saying, "I want you to give me at once the head of John the Baptist on a platter." And the king was exceedingly sorry; but because of his oaths and his guests he did not want to break his word to her. And immediately the king sent a soldier of the guard and gave orders to bring his head. He went and beheaded him in prison, and brought his head on a platter, and gave it to the girl; and the girl gave it to her mother. When his disciples heard of it, they came and took his body, and laid it in a tomb (Mk. 6:19–29).

This is a grisly story of a woman's hate and a man's weakness. Herodias was a bitter woman who hated John because of his exposure of her evil, so she constantly worked to destroy him. But Herod somehow was attracted to John and listened to him. All this took place in that forbidding castle called Machaerus on the east side of the Dead Sea, the ruins of which are still there. You can visit the dungeons and see where the chains were fastened to the walls, and where undoubtedly John the Baptist was held prisoner. There in that remote fortress Herod gave a banquet for his court and the great men of Galilee. On that occasion, as we have this story, Salome danced before him and pleased him, and he vowed to her he would give her anything she wanted. At her mother's request, she asked for the head of John the Baptist, and it was brought in on a platter. Herod thus reveals the weakness of his character in all his actions here.

Mark has given us this account because it provides the reason why Jesus sent out the twelve disciples. When John was first arrested, Jesus began his own ministry in Galilee. Now that John is beheaded, Jesus sends out the twelve to continue John's ministry: the message of repentance—and to add to it another note: the authority and power to cast out demons and to heal the sick, to heal emotionally and spiritually, as well as physically, those who were afflicted by guilt and sin. So, gradually, as we trace the account through, we see the Lord teaching these disciples what is to be the full message of the gospel. They were ignorant men at this point. They knew nothing of his impending death or his resurrection; they knew nothing even of who he was. They only knew that God was at work in Israel, that men were to come to a place of acknowledgment of need, and then God would begin to work in their lives. Little by little these other elements are being added as we go along. So you have a contrast here between the ministry of the twelve and the ministry of John.

Period of Danger

In the last two incidents here, we have what follows upon the return of the twelve from their mission, which includes the story of the feeding of the five thousand. We will see how that fits into this pattern in a moment, but first we have the result of the return of the twelve:

> The apostles returned to Jesus, and told him all that they had done and taught. And he said to them, "Come away by yourselves to a lonely place, and rest a while." For many were coming and going, and they had no leisure even to eat (Mk. 6:30–31).

It is clear from this that our Lord recognized this as a period of danger to these disciples. They needed rest, and he made provision for it. They needed time to think through what had happened. From reading Matthew's and Luke's accounts of this return, we know that these disciples were very excited by their ministry. They were tremendously encouraged by the results they had seen, and they came back like boys let out of school, eager to report to Jesus everything that had happened. They were so "turned on" and excited about it that he had to caution them, "Don't rejoice over the fact that the demons are subject to you, but rejoice rather that your names are written in heaven." He could see that they were in danger of being caught up with pride and exaltation at the ministry they had had. This, by the way, is the first time in the Gospels they are ever called "apostles." They had been "disciples" up to now, but now they had been "sent out"—that is what an apostle is, one who is sent out. They had been given a ministry of their own.

There is a very important principle of pedagogy here. For years churches have operated on the widely accepted principle that people must be thoroughly trained before you can put them to work. You have to stuff their heads full of knowledge and get them to answer all the great, tough theological questions. They have to be able to tell why God does not kill the devil, and who the anti-christ is, and solve many other knotty problems, before they are ready to go out and minister. When they have a degree from a seminary, or that equivalent, then they are finally ready to go to work.

Our Lord did not work that way. He sent out these ignorant men who did not by any means understand the fullness of the message they were preaching, who really had no idea why they were going out or what they were doing. But he sent them out, gave them power to act, and expected them to learn as they went. This is the way we ought to operate in our churches today. This principle, when applied, proves to be true; you do not wait until you know it all before you act. Rather, you start acting *as* you are learning; you learn as you go. This is what our Lord did with these men.

Nevertheless, when people are immature, the early success they enjoy tends to puff them up and exalt them and it becomes a very dangerous time in their lives. It is always a time of great peril when you have had success. I have learned this in my own ministry. Last week I received an invitation to be the Bible teacher at a major national conference to be held later this year. Immediately my flesh grabbed hold of that invitation and ran around the room of my mind, waving it and saying, "Look at this! All these people think you're a great Bible teacher!" And I began to anticipate what some of the results might be.

But my will, prompted by the Holy Spirit, rose right up, grabbed hold of that arrogant, vain young man, slammed him down in his seat, and told him, "Sit down and be quiet!" I realized that this was a time of great peril, of grave danger—a time to take it very thoughtfully and carefully and to remember that God works only through a humble and contrite spirit. Whenever any idea seizes the mind and heart that a ministry is for the glory of the individual, it is a serious threat to the whole success of the enterprise. This is why Jesus took these disciples off to a lonely place to minister to them and to teach them. But he had some difficulty doing it because the next passage says,

> And they went away in the boat to a lonely place by themselves. Now many saw them going, and knew them, and they ran there on foot from all the towns, and got there ahead of them. As he landed he saw a great throng, and he had compassion on them, because they were like sheep without a shepherd; and he began to teach them many things (Mk. 6:32–34).

I do not know how you would have reacted if you had been in Jesus' place. Here they were, trying to get away from the crowd, away from the pressure and the hassle and harassment of this ministry for a few quiet moments, arriving at the other side of the lake only to find waiting the same crowd they had just tried to get away from! I think I would have lost my temper and said, "Can't you leave us alone for one moment? We've got to have some time to rest. Don't you have any concern for us?" But notice how Jesus handles it. He had a shepherd's heart. Remember, it was he who said, "He who hungers and thirsts after righteousness *shall be filled.*" And here were men and women so hungry for the word of deliverance that, though he took a boat and rowed four miles across the lake, they ran ten miles by foot around the northern end of the lake and arrived at the other side before he got there! They were waiting there for him to teach them when he came. So without a word of rebuke, he began to teach them many things.

I do not know what he taught. Perhaps we have something of it in John's account where Jesus taught about the bread come down from heaven. Or in Luke's account where we have what we call the Sermon on the Mount, because it is a passage parallel to that in Matthew, although Luke says it was given on a plain. Perhaps our Lord repeated much of his Sermon on the Mount here to these people. But, whatever he taught, Mark goes on to tell us that he did a deliberate but amazing thing:

> And when it grew late, his disciples came to him and said, "This is a lonely place, and the hour is now late; send them away, to go into the country and villages round about and buy themselves something to eat." But he answered them, "You give them something to eat." And they said to him, "Shall we go and buy two hundred denarii worth of bread, and give it to them to eat?" And he said to them, "How many loaves have you? Go and see." [This was when Andrew found the boy who had a lunch with him.] And when they had found out, they said, "Five, and two fish." Then he commanded them all to sit down by companies upon the green grass. So they sat down in groups, by hundreds and by fifties (Mk. 6:35–40).

This is a very vivid description. It undoubtedly reflects Peter's memory of this event, which he related to Mark. This is the only miracle, by the way, which is recorded in all four Gospels. They never forgot this—Peter especially. He even remembered the green grass which was growing all over the hills and fields in the month of April when this took place, and that, as the people sat down, they looked like a vegetable garden. The word translated "groups" here is the word used for rows of vegetables in a garden. He could still see them, sitting on the hillside, lined up like vegetables in a row, waiting . . .

> And taking the five loaves and the two fish he looked up to heaven, and blessed, and broke the loaves, and gave them to the disciples to set before the people; and he divided the two fish among them all. And they all ate and were satisfied. And they took up twelve baskets full of broken pieces and of the

fish. And those who ate the loaves were five thousand men (Mk. 6:41–44).

I am sure you have studied this miracle and heard many messages based on this text. But I would simply like to point out three things about it. First, this was a deliberate action of our Lord. These people were not so hungry that he had to feed them. Later on, when he fed the four thousand, they had been without food for three days. But here it is questionable that they had been without food even for a full day. They had run around the lake and were very tired, perhaps, but not overly hungry.

Lessons for Blind Disciples

Nevertheless, he chose to feed them, and he did so, secondly, in order to teach his disciples something. This was primarily for their benefit. What he did was designed to remind them of the feeding of the multitudes of Israel in the wilderness when the manna came down from heaven. He was drawing a deliberate picture of who he was for these disciples. This is why John's Gospel records that he said to them, "I am the bread come down from heaven." These disciples were expected to learn from this something of who it was they were following. But they seemed to miss the point.

There is a hint given here for them, thirdly, that this event was related somehow to God's whole ministry to Israel. Mark says, ". . . they took up twelve baskets full of broken pieces . . ." Whenever the number twelve is used in these stories, it relates to the twelve tribes of Israel. Jesus himself said he chose twelve disciples so that they might sit upon twelve thrones judging the twelve tribes of Israel. In the previous section there was a dying girl who was twelve years old and a woman who had had an issue of blood for twelve years. Now there are twelve baskets of food taken up. This is a reminder to these disciples that Jesus was the Promised One who was to come to Israel. He was the Provider sent by God. He had provided rest for his disciples, had provided truth for the multitude waiting, and had provided food for these people. But their eyes were shut.

So another incident immediately follows, one which is very important:

> Immediately he made his disciples get into the boat and go before him to the other side, to Bethsaida, while he dismissed the crowd. And after he had taken leave of them, he went into the hills to pray. And when evening came, the boat was out on the sea, and he was alone on the land. And he saw that they were distressed in rowing, for the wind was against them. And about the fourth watch of the night [about three or four o'clock in the morning] he came to them, walking on the sea. He meant to pass by them, but when they saw him walking on the sea they thought it was a ghost, and cried out; for they all saw him, and were terrified. But immediately he spoke to them and said, "Take heart, it is I; have no fear." And he got into the boat with them and the wind ceased. And they were utterly astounded, for they did not understand about the loaves, but their hearts were hardened (Mk. 6:45–52).

We cannot understand this last miracle except as we see it as a kind of examination given to these disciples after the feeding of the five thousand. Our Lord had sent them out, had given them power. They had seen their ministry confirmed and authenticated by the hand of God working through them. They had come back excited and "turned on" by all they had seen and done. They had now been taught that Jesus was the One who was coming to fulfill the expectation of a Messiah to be given to Israel, promised throughout all the prophetic centuries. But somehow they seemed to miss it all.

So he gives them an examination, a test, to see how they are doing. He sends them out into a storm. This time it is different.

He is not with them in the boat. He sends them out alone, deliberately, and he goes up into the hills to pray. How many storms of our life are made up of these two elements—trouble which comes to us and seems to be overwhelming us, and the seeming absence of the Lord? Nevertheless, there is One up on the hillside praying for us.

After the storm has blown for several hours and the disciples are in deep distress, Jesus comes to them walking upon the water. When they see him, they are scared out of their wits. They think it is a ghost. He has to reassure them, "It—that thing you see which scares you to death—it is I; don't be afraid." How many times does he have to say that to us? That thing which scares us, frightens us—"It is I; be not afraid." He got into the boat, and Mark says they were absolutely flabbergasted! This indicates the grade they got on this exam. It was "F"—F for fear, and F for flabbergasted. It was a total failure, but it astonished them. For the second time, now, their eyes are opened to begin to question, "Who then is this? Who is it?" And they begin to listen. This opens the door for some of our Lord's greatest teaching to his disciples regarding why he came.

And this is our Lord's question to us: "Who is this?" Who sends the storms into our lives? Who tests us? Who makes provision for our needs and then tests us on it? Who gives us a promise and then sends us out to see if we believe what we teach or what we say? It is the Lord himself. This is what he is doing with us, as he did with his disciples. He is training us, teaching us, preparing us, building into our lives, as he built into their lives, so that we might be men and women of faith—confident and calm and able to cope with life.

12

When Rite Is Wrong

If you have ever seen "Fiddler On The Roof," you may remember how Tevye, the leading character, opens with the song, "Tradition!" The whole Jewish community was built upon and governed by the long-standing, unbreakable traditions of the past. The unspoken thesis of that play and movie is the way these traditions were being challenged by the unrest and uprootings of the day, and that when tradition is violated grief and hardship often ensue. This is suggestive of the scene before us now as Mark draws the stark contrast between the ministry of Jesus, who is reaching out in healing love to men and women all over the region, and the hindering work of the scribes and the Pharisees, armed with tradition, who try to halt that ministry of love. Thomas Dixon, one of the great preachers of the last century, once said, "Tradition was the most constant, the most persistent, the most dogged, the most utterly devilish opposition the Master encountered. It openly attacked him on every hand, and silently repulsed his teaching." That is what we will be seeing in this passage. With the closing words of chapter

6, Mark describes for us something more of the healing ministry of our Lord:

> And when they had crossed over [the Sea of Galilee], they came to land at Gennesaret, and moored to the shore. And when they got out of the boat, immediately the people recognized him, and ran about the whole neighborhood and began to bring sick people on their pallets to any place where they heard he was. And wherever he came, in villages, cities, or country, they laid the sick in the market places, and besought him that they might touch even the fringe of his garment; and as many as touched it were made well (Mk. 6:53–56).

This is a beautiful scene in the ministry of Jesus. As you can see, the story of the woman with the issue of blood who was healed by touching the hem of Jesus' garment has spread now throughout all the regions around Galilee. So wherever Jesus appears, instantly the people begin to bring out the sick and the diseased and the demon-possessed, "that they might touch even the fringe of his garment." And, as Mark tells us, ". . . as many as touched it were made well." This is a wonderful fulfillment of that beautiful poetic prediction in one of the most majestic passages of Isaiah the prophet:

> Then the eyes of the blind shall be opened, and the ears of the deaf unstopped; then shall the lame man leap like a hart, and the tongue of the dumb sing for joy (Isa. 35:5–6).

We can see this in Mark's beautifully descriptive account, as our Lord fulfilled those other words of Isaiah, which Matthew quotes: "He took our infirmities and bore our diseases."

In deliberate contrast to that, Mark immediately moves to the story of a delegation of Pharisees and scribes:

> Now when the Pharisees gathered together to him, with some of the scribes, who had come from Jerusalem, they saw that

some of his disciples ate with hands defiled, that is, unwashed.
(For the Pharisees, and all the Jews, do not eat unless they
wash their hands, observing the tradition of the elders; and when
they come from the market place, they do not eat unless they
purify themselves [Some versions read "baptize themselves,"
i.e., wash all over]; and there are many other traditions which
they observe, the washing of cups and pots and vessels of
bronze) (Mk. 7:1–4).

This introduces us to the subject of the power and effect of
tradition. In this opening paragraph we see something of the
tremendous force which tradition plays in our lives. Not only
was this true of them in that day; it is true of us today. Some of
us go to church, for instance, because it is traditional; Sunday is
the day you go to church. All your life you have gone to church
on Sunday. Or we have sung certain hymns because they are
traditional in a morning worship service. We will do many such
things because it is traditional! This power from the past
touches us all at one time or another. Now, is it good, or is it
bad? We will learn in this passage, from the lips of Jesus, the
element which makes tradition either good or evil.

Notice that this delegation from Jerusalem was motivated by
the deliberate intent of antagonizing Jesus. Evidently word of
this spreading popular movement had reached Jerusalem, and
the chief priests and rulers of the Jews were troubled about it.
As we have just seen, it had already reached the ears of Herod.
So a delegation of Pharisees and scribes came down from Jerusalem with the specific intention of finding something in the
ministry of Jesus with which they could oppose him. They knew
that if they could find some way in which Jesus challenged the
popularly accepted traditions, they could turn the crowd against
him. This tells us how strongly these traditions were held.

Ritual Washing

The one they chose was this: As they watched the disciples
and Jesus, they saw that some did not wash their hands in the

prescribed way before they ate. This does not mean they were dirty disciples who never bothered to wash their hands before they ate. This is not a problem of hygiene at all. I am sure they did wash their hands before they ate. But what bothered the Pharisees was that they did not do it in the right way. You see, among the Jews, you could have washed your hands with the finest of soaps and scrubbed like a doctor preparing for surgery; but if you did not do it in a certain way, you were just as unclean, ceremonially, as though you had not washed at all.

In the Revised Standard Version there is a marginal note which says that one word in verse 3—in the phrase "wash their hands"—is of uncertain meaning and is not translated. It is the word for "fist." The translators evidently had difficulty understanding how this word fit into the context. But scholars tell us that it was the rigid custom among the Jews to wash in this way: The hands had to be held out, palms up, hands cupped slightly, and water poured over them. Then the fist of one hand was used to scrub the other, and then the other fist would scrub the first hand. This is why the fist is mentioned here. Finally, the hands again were held out, with palms down, and water was poured over them a second time to cleanse away the dirty water the defiled hands had been scrubbed with. Only then would a person's hands be ceremonially clean. He might not even have been hygienically clean, but he would have been ceremonially clean. That is, he would have been considered acceptable to God, having given strict attention to the prescribed ritual of cleansing and thus would have been able to eat in a proper manner. So strongly was this ingrained in them that when one rabbi was imprisoned by the Romans for an offense he used the drinking water brought to him in his solitary dungeon cell to wash his hands in this way. He almost died of thirst! That is how important it was to them to observe these traditions.

Now, the traditions had begun in right ways. That is, they were simply an attempt to understand the Law. The Book of Leviticus did require that certain ablutions, certain washings, be performed as a way of teaching the people how to handle sin. That was the intent of the Law. But as these requirements were applied to various situations, certain suggestions were made as to the proper way to do it. And there was nothing wrong with that, particularly. But then the priests began to interpret the suggestions which had been made, and to add to them. Then interpretations of the interpretations were added until gradually there was built up a tremendous mass of tradition which demanded inflexible obedience and scrupulous observance of even the minor details, so that the purpose of the Law was forgotten.

This is what has happened in the Christian church. In the Book of Acts you find an amazing liberty of the Spirit among the people of God. The Lord never worked twice in the same way in the Book of Acts. That is beautiful to see. But you cannot deduce a ceremony or a ritual for the church from the Book of Acts, because God is moving in freshness and variety and spontaneity wherever you turn. But soon some of these ways were settled upon as *the* right way to do a thing, and others were added, and interpretations were added to them, until through the years, as you well know, there have grown up varying categories of worship forms—"orders of service" we call them—each claiming to be *the* right one. Many of us have been victims of these. We do not feel we have worshiped unless we have sung the Gloria Patri or read the Apostles' Creed or something similar. This is what our Lord is dealing with. Mark shows us first of all the force of such tradition in these people's lives.

In the next section, we read the words of Jesus with regard to tradition:

And the Pharisees and the scribes asked him, "Why do your disciples not live according to the tradition of the elders, but eat with hands defiled?" And he said to them, "Well did Isaiah prophesy of you hypocrites, as it is written, 'This people honors me with their lips, but their heart is far from me; in vain do

they worship me, teaching as doctrines the precepts of men'"
(Mk. 7:5–7).

Those are very insightful words. With our Lord's keen per-
ceptiveness, he plunges right to the heart of the issue. When
the Pharisees ask him, "Why do your disciples not observe the
traditions?" he points out to them, first of all, the effect that the
observance of tradition has upon our lives. It produces hypocrites. "You hypocrites," he says. I am sometimes amazed as I
read through the Gospels at the bluntness of the language of
Jesus! In fact, Matthew's account tells us that the disciples said
to him afterward, "Do you realize that you offended those Pharisees?" And he did offend them, deliberately, with full knowledge of what he was doing.

But notice what he is doing here. He is pointing out the result of traditional "worship." And he utilizes the word of the
prophet Isaiah to show us what it is like. There are two kinds of
hypocrisy, according to Isaiah. First, there is that which consists
of right words but wrong attitudes. Everything outward is right,
but inwardly the mind and heart are wrong. That, Jesus says, is
hypocrisy—to look as if you are doing something religious and
worshipful and God-related, but inside to have an entirely different attitude.

A few years ago, when the youth revolt first began on the
West Coast, many of us were puzzled and offended when young
people would say to us, in one way or another, "We don't want
to come to church because churches are filled with hypocrites."
Some of us could not understand what they meant. We knew
there might be *some* churches that were filled with hypocrites,
but not *ours!* We had honest difficulty with this. We could not
see where there was any hypocrisy in a thoroughly Bible-
centered, evangelical church such as ours. But what they were
saying was this: "You use great words, wonderful words ('God-
words' they called them)—but you don't really mean them.
You talk about love, but you don't love. You talk about for-

giveness, but you don't forgive. You talk about acceptance, but you don't accept." And they were right.

Externalized Religion

That is what tradition does to us. It externalizes religion, makes it outward instead of inward. As long as we are fulfilling the prescribed outward form, we think we are acceptable before God. That is the terrible danger of tradition. This particular form which Isaiah mentions here—right words and wrong attitudes—is widespread among Christians. We all suffer from it, and we ought to recognize it and admit it. It is a struggle we all have, without exception. And it has resulted in what is probably the most deadly danger to the evangelistic message of the church—the self-righteousness of Christians, thinking that because we do things in the "right" way and say the "right" words and believe the "right" doctrines, we are thus pleasing to God.

I have a Christian friend, a very intelligent, sharp-minded businessman, who has an extremely vivid imagination. One day he sent me an article he had written and asked me to comment on it. I have held on to a copy of it ever since and share it with you here because it is such a beautiful statement of the danger of this self-righteousness within the church.

DON'T TAKE ME TO THE HOSPITAL, PLEASE!

This scene didn't make sense. There he lay in the street, bleeding—the hit-and-run driver gone. He needed medical help immediately! Yet he kept pleading, "Don't take me to the hospital, please!" Surprised, everyone asked why. Pleadingly, he answered, "Because I'm on the *staff* at the hospital. It would be *embarrassing* for them to see me like this. They've *never* seen me bleeding and dirty. They always see me clean and healthy; now I'm a *mess.*"

"But the hospital is *for* people like you! Can't we call an ambulance?" "No, please don't. I took a Pedestrian Safety Course, and the instructor would *criticize* me for getting hit."

"But who *cares* what the instructor thinks? You need attention." "But there are other reasons, too. The Admissions Clerk would be upset." "Well, why?" "Because she always gets upset if anyone for admittance doesn't have all the details she needs to fill out her records. I didn't see who hit me, and I don't even know the make of the car or the license number. She wouldn't *understand*. She's a real stickler for records. Worse than that, I haven't got my Blue Cross Card."

"What real difference would that make?" "Well, if they didn't recognize me in this mess, they wouldn't let me in. They won't admit anyone in my shape without a Blue Cross card. They must be sure it isn't going to *cost* the institution. They protect the institution. Just pull me over to the curb. I'll make it some way. It's my fault that I got hit."

With this, he tried to crawl to the gutter while everyone left, leaving him alone. Maybe he made it, maybe he didn't. Maybe he's still trying to stop his own bleeding.

Does that strike you as a strange, ridiculous story? It could happen any Sunday in a typical church membership. I *know* it could happen, because last night I asked some active Christians what they would do if on Saturday night they got hit and run over by some unacceptable sin. Without exception they said, "I sure wouldn't want to go to church the next morning, where everybody would see me."

Now, be honest—would you? Or would you reason, "The members would ostracize me. They would look at me like I was strange, and didn't belong there any more. Some of the self-righteous would accuse me of being a hypocrite. The Sunday school teacher would be mad at me for not learning what had been taught. Those sitting next to me would be embarrassed, not knowing how to react because they didn't know how everybody else felt. They really wouldn't know how to react to a known dirty saint."

In the good-natured spirit of the conversation we decided, if caught—hit and run over—by some unacceptable sin, we would be better off to go to the pool hall instead of to the church. At the pool hall we would find sympathy, real understanding. Immediately, someone would say, "This isn't the end of the world.

It happened to me, and I lived through it." Another would say,
"I see you slipped and got caught. Well, don't let it get you
down. I know a good lawyer who will help you." Another would
add, "You really seem more like one of us than you did before.
Now we know you're just like us."

Now, the question that bothered us is: Where should real love
and understanding live—in the pool hall or in the church of
Jesus Christ, who died for sinners? Is the church really going to
be the church until every Christian, hit and run over by some sin,
starts pleading, "Take me to the church. My brothers and sisters
are there. They care for me. I can get well there. I'm a weak
member of the Body, but when I hurt, the strong members favor
me. And I don't need a paid-up Blue Cross card. And I know
they won't talk about me when it's over." Yet, to the last single
person at the party, there was not one who said he would feel
welcome in his church if the night before he had been caught in
some sin which had become known.

That is what our Lord is warning us about here.

Isaiah tells us there is a second form of hypocrisy: "In vain
do they worship me, teaching as doctrines the precepts of men."
This is widespread in the church, too. It is the idea that if we
take the principles and the precepts by which the world operates
—dog-eat-dog, every man for himself, fulfill yourself first, etc.,
and clothe them with the words of Scripture, then we are worshiping God. But Jesus says that is hypocrisy and is a failure to
worship.

What, then, *is* worship? If it is not something you do outwardly, then what is it? Our Lord put his finger on what, in my
judgment, is the greatest definition of worship when he said to
the woman at the well, "God is spirit, and those who worship
him must worship in spirit and truth" (John 4:24). That says
three things. First, worship must be genuine. It must be something you do inside of you which is deep and real. It cannot be
superficial, it cannot be shallow, it cannot be something done
with the mind but not with the heart—with your emotions dis-

engaged from what your mind is doing. Anything less than full involvement of mind, emotions, and will is hypocrisy.

Second, worship is individual. In a sense, we cannot have public worship. We can participate in a service together corporately, but worship is only what is going on inside of you. It is "in spirit"—*your* spirit. It is your attitude toward the greatness and glory of God, your response to his goodness and his truth. It has nothing to do with what your body is doing at the moment, whether it is bowing, or closing your eyes, or saying certain words. God is looking for those who will worship him in spirit and in truth. And since it is individual, it is varied. That is, one will be reacting in one way, at one level, another at another level. Thus, we can expect it to manifest itself in varied ways, with various expressions. That is why it is wrong to have one set way of expressing worship and one set time to do it, and never to change.

This is reinforced in the third thing our Lord brought out here: worship must be realistic, i.e., according to the way we understand truth, reality. This means it is growing. Worship must change. It cannot remain static because our knowledge of reality changes. The more we know, the more different ways we will worship. In a sense, all the church can do on Sunday mornings is to provide an opportunity for you to worship. *You* must worship; all the leaders of the service can do is to provide an occasion for you to do so. Worship, therefore, is something which goes on in the human heart all the time—at least, it can and should.

Look at what our Lord says next. He has shown us the danger of tradition—hypocrisy; now we have the course of its development beginning with verse 8:

"You leave the commandment of God, and hold fast the tradition of men." And he said to them, "You have a fine way of rejecting the commandment of God, in order to keep your tradition! For Moses said, 'Honor your father and your mother'; and, 'He who speaks evil of father or mother, let him surely die'; but you say, 'If a man tells his father or his mother, what you would have gained from me is Corban' (that is, given to God)—then you no longer permit him to do anything for his father or mother, thus making void the word of God through your tradition which you hand on. And many such things you do" (Mk. 7:8–13).

In those incisive words our Lord is tracing for us what happens when tradition begins to gain sway. First, it begins with leaving the command of God. Traditions arise when in some way we try to find a substitute to give God, instead of what he really wants. A businessman told me of a Christian friend who had invited him out to lunch and had said to him, "I don't know what's wrong. Everything is going wrong in my life. I'm about to lose my business; our whole financial base is collapsing! And I don't understand why, because for years I've given money to God, faithfully—given him vast amounts of money. I've put that first! And yet, everything is falling apart." My friend said to him, "Did you ever stop to think that what God wants is not your money, but you?" This is where hypocrisy begins—with leaving the command of God.

It is interesting that the Greek word used here for "tradition" is the word for surrender, giving up, or substitution. God says, "I want you." But you say, "Would you mind just taking this instead—my money, my time, my wife, my children, my interests? But don't touch me!" That is where tradition begins—by leaving the command of God and offering a substitute, holding fast the tradition of men. The substitute is always something "good"; we would never think of offering God something bad! But it is not what he wants.

Clever Rejection

The second step, as our Lord indicates here, is to deny and injure both God and man. He illustrates with a word about fathers and mothers. The Law says, "Honor your father and your mother." That means more than being courteous to them; it means taking care of them, especially as they grow older. The Jews had worked out a keen little way—a "neat" way, Jesus called it—of rejecting the commandment of God. He almost congratulates them on their cleverness. They took the money which should have been spent on their father and mother and said, "This is a gift to God," dedicated it to God, and then they were free to use it themselves. Their parents could not touch it because it was "dedicated" to God. The modern equivalent is to erect a tax shelter. I do not mean that all tax shelters are wrong. But they can be, and often are, a way of setting aside money which ought to be used for other purposes and saying, "You can't touch it. I'm sorry. I've got it all tied up in a tax shelter and therefore God has no claim upon me in this regard." Jesus exposes all that. He tells us we will end up hurting people when we do that.

One man I know told me recently how concerned he is about certain missionary couples who have "dedicated themselves to God" to such a degree that they neglect their families, ship their children off to school, abandon their responsibilities in the home, and excuse it all by saying, "We're dedicating ourselves to the work of God." That is "Corban," and that is hypocrisy.

Our Lord proceeds even further, and, beginning with verse 14, gives us the source of tradition:

> And he called the people to him again, and said to them, "Hear me, all of you, and understand: there is nothing outside a man which by going into him can defile him; but the things which come out of a man are what defile him." And when he had entered the house, and left the people, his disciples asked him about the parable. And he said to them, "Then are you also without understanding? Do you not see that whatever goes into a man from outside cannot defile him, since it enters, not his heart but his stomach, and so passes on?" (Thus he declared all foods clean.) And he said, "What comes out of a man is what defiles a man. For from within, out of the heart of man, come

evil thoughts, fornication, theft, murder, adultery, coveting, wickedness, deceit, licentiousness, envy, slander, pride, foolishness. [All the excrement of the mind and heart is what defiles.] All these evil things come from within, and they defile a man" (Mk. 7:14-23).

What he is saying about these customs is that there is nothing inherently wrong about them, and nothing inherently good; what you do outwardly is neither bad nor good. What you are thinking and feeling and how you are reacting inside is what determines whether it is bad or good. A practice can be perfectly wholesome and healthy if the spirit is worshiping. Corporate "worship" apart from that is evil and degenerate, rotten and defiled in the sight of God. And he puts his finger on the source of this evil within us. Of course, what he is saying here is that all of us are fallen creatures, *and our flesh remains* a fallen creature as long as we are in this life. This is what the Scriptures tell us again and again. Becoming Christians means that we have a way of overcoming these evils, so we do not need to act out of this kind of thinking. But it does not mean that we will ever in this life be free from the temptations and the urges of these defilements which are listed here.

Something for Everyone

This is very important for us to know. It is what delivers Christians from being self-righteous snobs—when we realize that what our Lord has outlined here is true of every single one of us. Do not go through this list and pick out the things you do not do. What Jesus is saying to you is, "If you are guilty of one of them, you are capable of all of them." You need only the proper circumstances to show you how true that is. To quote my friend again, his paper goes on to say,

I remember one of the most saintly women I've ever known, who startled me, by saying, "There isn't a sin of which I am not capable. I could be a prostitute, I could be a murderess, I could embezzle." I was convinced she couldn't. Instead, I thought she was displaying a large humility, and, therefore, I congratulated her on it. But she caught me up short. "You don't really believe I mean that. I do mean it, because I realize that if there is a person who has committed a single sin of which I feel incapable, then I am not able to love that person. The same sin that crops up in their life, in their form, also flows through me and expresses itself in other ways. Until I believe that, I am a self-righteous, proud, arrogant woman."

That is putting it bluntly, but in the terms our Lord himself has stated for us. There is no difference, then, in any of us; we are all alike. Only the redemptive process of God frees us from this at any given moment. These evil things pervade the human heart, and this is what defiles us in the sight of God. Nothing we can do outwardly makes it any better or any worse; the change must come within.

Mark goes on to bring into immediate conjunction with this incident another story. It may look at first as though he has changed the subject. But he has not at all, as we shall see:

And from there he arose and went away to the region of Tyre and Sidon. And he entered a house, and would not have any one know it; yet he could not be hid. But immediately a woman, whose little daughter was possessed by an unclean spirit, heard of him, and came and fell down at his feet. Now the woman was a Greek, a Syrophoenician by birth. And she begged him to cast the demon out of her daughter. And he said to her, "Let the children first be fed, for it is not right to take the children's bread and throw it to the dogs." [Here he used a diminutive, a term which means "pets," not scruffy street dogs.] But she answered him, "Yes, Lord; yet even the dogs [pets] under the table eat the children's crumbs." And he said to her, "For this saying you may go your way; the demon has left your daughter." And she went home, and found the child lying in bed, and the demon gone (Mk. 7:24–30).

Two questions are always asked about this incident. The first is, "Why did Jesus go into Tyre and Sidon?" These were gentile cities, Canaanite cities. Matthew tells that this woman was a Canaanite. Yet Jesus left immediately after his teaching on tradition and went into Tyre and Sidon. Why? The only answer is that, as we have seen in this whole section of Mark, he is teaching his disciples certain lessons. He was illustrating in terms of race what he had just said in terms of food. All foods are clean and all peoples are clean in the sense of being accepted by God. There are no distinctions among foods, as being defiling or undefiling; there are also no distinctions among people. So he led them to a gentile city in order that their Jewish scruples might be challenged immediately.

Tradition vs. Faith

The second question is, "Why did he treat this woman rather harshly?" Matthew says that when she first asked him to heal her daughter, he would not even answer her. Many have wondered why. I think the answer is in Matthew's account, where we are told that she first addressed him in this way: "O thou Son of David, come and heal my daughter." "Son of David" is a Jewish term for the Jewish Messiah. She was coming to him on the ground that he was a Jew and she was a gentile. That is why he said to her, "The children first must be fed," because it was God's program that this gospel go to the Jews first and then to the gentiles. Now, he never intended that the gentiles be excluded. But it was to be in the order of the Jews first, then the gentiles. And when she came on that ground, invoking all the power of Jewish tradition, he said to her, in effect, "You will have to wait until the time comes, until the gospel goes out to the gentiles. Then I can heal your daughter. By coming on this ground, you have imposed limits and barriers on God. Until they are removed, you cannot come."

But then we have this refreshing change. The woman, concerned about her daughter, in agony for her child, presses through and says, "Yes, Lord; I know that's right. The children ought to eat first, and then the dogs. But even the dogs eat the crumbs which fall from the children's table." Then she said what Matthew records: "Lord, help me." The minute she turned from the ground of tradition and the Hebrew approach and, merely as a needy woman concerned about her child, said, "Lord, help me," our Lord's answer was immediate: "Go your way, your daughter is healed." By this incident Mark wants us to learn that tradition is a way of building barriers between us and God. But faith strikes through them all right to the heart of God. When we come to God in simple faith, without any form or ritual or prescribed words—merely open our spirit in its need before a providing God—the answer is always instant and immediate, and healing comes. That is why we worship by our inner response, by what we think while we are singing and praying, rather than by the outward form.

Are you worshiping God now, this moment? Is your spirit open to him, recognizing an immediate relationship to him which has nothing to do with whether you are sitting or standing or bowing or singing or praying? Do you come to him as a child of God, admitting your need and responding to his provision for that need with a thankful heart so that your whole person is involved—spirit, mind, will, emotions, and body in their right and proper order? Not emotions first, not physical actions first, but responding as a whole person in spirit and in truth? That is when you are worshiping God, and the Father seeks such to worship him.

13

Do You Not Yet Understand?

In the passage we come to now, Jesus continues his ministry among the gentiles as he pursues his goal of instructing the twelve as to who he is. Perhaps it is startling to realize that Jesus spent almost a third of his three-year ministry among gentiles. This fact has been obscured by the emphasis upon his ministry among the Jews. But obviously he was seeking to impart to his disciples some sense of his mission and ministry to the gentile world as well as to the Jews. We begin with the account in Mark 7:31, an account of his travels through the region on the eastern side of the Sea of Galilee:

> Then he returned from the region of Tyre, and went through Sidon to the Sea of Galilee, through the region of the Decapolis. And they brought to him a man who was deaf and had an impediment in his speech; and they besought him to lay his hand upon him. And taking him aside from the multitude privately, he put his fingers into his ears, and he spat and touched his tongue; and looking up to heaven, he sighed, and said to him, "Eph-phatha," that is, "Be opened." And his ears were opened, his tongue was released, and he spoke plainly (Mk. 7:31–35).

Mark is careful to tell us this took place in the area called the Decapolis, the ten Greek cities on the eastern side of the Sea of Galilee. And he points out that Jesus went into this region in a rather strange way. Instead of coming directly back into Galilee, he left Tyre and Sidon and went by a northern route through what is now the country of Syria and continued down the eastern side of the Sea of Galilee into the southern part of that region. It would be very much like starting out for Los Angeles from San Francisco and going by way of Reno and Las Vegas. Many scholars feel that this journey took about eight months, so that he spent a long time in the gentile regions ministering to those who were not Jews. We can see that on the way he is very much involved in teaching his disciples what he wants them to learn. Here we have another of those little incidents which represent our Lord's reminder to the twelve, and to us, of the indispensability of faith. We must act in faith toward God. That is the thrust of the healing of this man who was deaf and dumb.

When you consider it, the condition of this man was pitiful. When I was a boy, I felt that the worst thing that could happen to me would be to become blind. I felt sorry for blind people and was fearful that some accident would take my sight. But through the years since I have come to realize that much more to be pitied are those who are deaf and dumb, for they are shut off from society even more completely than the blind. This man was both deaf and dumb. He could not hear; he could not speak. Therefore, he could not read, and thus was shut away from the light of God in the Scriptures. He could not hear a testimony; he could not ask any questions; he was living in a silent world of complete isolation from all those around him. Thus he represents a very difficult kind of person to reach.

This explains what our Lord did with this man. First, he took him aside privately. Those who are deaf have told me that it is embarrassing to be deaf, because no one can see your difficulty. If you were blind or lame, they could see it and make allowances. But if you are deaf, no one can see it, and it is embarrassing to ask people to shout at you or repeat what they have said. So, out of consideration for this man, in the tenderness of his heart, our Lord leads him aside from the multitude to deal with him privately.

To Awaken Faith

There he did some unusual things: he put his fingers into the man's ears. Then he spat on his fingers and touched the man's tongue. Then, looking into the heavens, he sighed—all this before he said the wonderful word, "Be opened." I confess that it is only in this current study in the Gospel of Mark that I have begun to understand why he did this. Unquestionably, it is because he is seeking to arouse and awaken this man's faith. And in order to do so, he acts out what he wants to convey to him. He puts his fingers into his ears to indicate to the man that he intends to heal them. He wets his fingers and touches the man's tongue to indicate that he is going to heal the tongue and that words will flow freely from it. He looks up into heaven to indicate that the power for this must come from God. And he sighs —not so much a sigh as a breathing out—to convey to the man that it is by the invisible agency of the power of God that he will be made well.

When Jesus could see in his eyes the response, the look of faith, the look of comprehension of what he intended to do, then he said the word: "Eph-phatha," the Aramaic word which Peter undoubtedly preserved in telling Mark of this incident. It means, "Be opened," and the man immediately began to hear and to speak. That is amazing, for those who recover their hearing after a long period of silence usually cannot speak but must learn how. This man instantly began to speak. This was our Lord's way of showing us and the disciples who were watching that faith is a necessary ingredient to receiving anything from God. Faith—believing in the activity of an invisible God who, nevertheless, despite the fact that you cannot see him, is ready to work in your life. So he awakened this man's faith and caused him to believe in the invisible. This is the essential to all divine activity among men.

Two Different Levels

Immediately he begins to take steps to prevent the abuse of this miracle:

And he charged them to tell no one; but the more he charged them, the more zealously they proclaimed it. And they were astonished beyond measure, saying, "He has done all things well; he even makes the deaf hear and the dumb speak" (Mk. 7:36–37).

Notice the change in pronouns here. Jesus, up to this point, has been dealing with the man as an individual. But now he suddenly speaks to the crowd and charges them to tell no one. The Greek verb tense indicates that he kept on telling them, repeatedly. Perhaps several times he said to them, "Do not spread this abroad." But the more he charged them, the more zealously they kept on proclaiming it. They were beginning to go out into the countryside and tell of this exciting miracle. The reason our Lord did this, as on previous occasions, was to prevent a misemphasis. He did not want to become known as a wonder worker. The faith of this crowd and the faith of the man who was healed were on two different levels. The eyes of the crowd saw no further than the *actions of God.* They saw the miracle. The eyes of the man who was healed were fixed upon the *God who acts.* That is where faith must rest. So when this crowd, with its low level of understanding, its emphasis upon the merely spectacular, started to disperse, Jesus charged them, warned them, not to tell it abroad. But he did not say that to the man, for *his* eyes were fixed upon the God who is ready to act. And when your faith is fixed on that—not on what God does, but on who God is—then you are free to be a witness to those around you.

The account moves right on into chapter 8. Ignore the chapter break. I do not know who put these in, but they almost always come at the wrong place.

> In those days, when again a great crowd had gathered, and they had nothing to eat, he called his disciples to him, and said to them, "I have compassion on the crowd, because they have been with me now three days, and have nothing to eat; and if I send them away hungry to their homes, they will faint on the way; and some of them have come a long way." And his disciples answered him, "How can one feed these men with bread here in the desert?" And he asked them, "How many loaves have you?" They said, "Seven." And he commanded the crowd to sit down on the ground; and he took the seven loaves, and having given thanks he broke them and gave them to his disciples to set before the people; and they set them before the crowd. And they had a few small fish; and having blessed them, he commanded that these also should be set before them. And they ate, and were satisfied; and they took up the broken pieces left over, seven baskets full. And there were about four thousand people. And he sent them away . . . (Mk. 8:1–10).

There are similarities between this account and that of the feeding of the five thousand, which came somewhat earlier and occurred in the Jewish area of Galilee. But this is another account, of feeding four thousand, and in a different part of the country. Some commentators have tried to assert that these are but two different versions of the same incident. But both Matthew and Mark are careful to tell us there were two events like this. Jesus himself, as we will see a bit later, refers to the two different events as having significance in the lives of his apostles.

Yet these were very similar. Bread and fish were the foods in both cases, and our Lord multiplied them when they were brought to him. Why did he repeat this miracle? Perhaps part of the answer is that he was doing with the gentiles what he had also done among the Jews, so that these gentiles would be taught the same spiritual lessons as the Jews and the disciples would see that this was intended for gentiles as well.

But Mark makes clear that basically it arose from the compassion that Jesus had for these people. They had been with him for three days without any food. Now, it is without question that they came because they wanted to see the miracles he was doing. Just as he had anticipated, the spreading abroad of news of the healing of the deaf and dumb man had brought people streaming out of the cities. They were there to watch the wonder worker, the miracle man. For three days they had hung around, hoping that he would do a miracle. Probably our Lord taught them during that period. We do not know exactly what he taught—perhaps he repeated some of his earlier messages, as any good preacher would do when he had a different crowd before him. But they were not content with that, and had lingered, hoping to see a miracle. Finally, after three days, they knew they must return home. But Jesus is loathe to send them away with no food. He does not want to do any more miracles, lest they miss the real message. But he does, because of his compassionate heart. He does not want to send them back and have them faint along the way, so he decides to feed them.

Whatever You Have

As we read this account, we must ask ourselves, "What did he want these disciples to learn from this?" Because what he wanted them to learn is what he wants us to learn. This is why it is recorded for us here on these pages. Some things are very obvious. First, he wanted them to learn to begin with what they had. When you want God to act, do not wait for God to do everything, because he expects us to be involved in the work that he does. Start with what you have. When he said he was going to feed the crowd and they asked how he was going to do it out there in the desert, his first words were, "How many loaves do you have?" They checked around, and said, "Seven." He said, "That will do. Any amount—whatever you have. Just start with what you have."

Many of us want God to do things in our lives. We pray that he will work in various ways. And it is right that we should ask him to work. There are things he can do that we cannot do at all. We can bring the bread, but he must multiply it. We can fill the jars with water, but he must turn it into wine. But start with what you have. Years ago I read of a young Christian who was in the first glow of relationship with God. He was walking along a country road one day, and he was very hungry. He prayed that God would supply him with food. Before he finished his prayer, a bread truck passed by and a loaf fell out the back end onto the road. But rather than running over and picking it up, this young man sat down and prayed, "Lord, if you intend that bread to be for me, then cause it to come through the air to me!" Our Lord would teach us that there are practical things we can do. Start with what you have. When you want to see something accomplished for God, begin where you are.

The second lesson our Lord clearly wanted them to learn is that the supply will always equal the demand. God will never quit giving as long as the need remains. It is wonderful the way this is put in the original Greek. Our translation says, ". . . he took the seven loaves, and . . . broke them"; but the English is faulty. What the Greek really says is, ". . . he kept on breaking them"—and the disciples kept on feeding the multitude. Jesus stood there at the front of the crowd, took the seven loaves, and began to break them. He did not build up a great pile of bread and another pile of fish and say, "Now take that and distribute it." No, he just handed it out a little at a time, but it kept on going, and going, and going—first the bread, and then the fish. They had plenty to feed everybody, but nothing visible as a resource from which to draw. God wants us to learn that is the way he acts in our lives.

Spiritual Hunger

Then he obviously wants to impart to them a very deeply needed lesson. Notice that all the Lord's miracles are always done on the physical level. But our Lord is never happy with their remaining at that level. We have seen this many times before. He does not want people to focus on the physical. He wants these disciples to see also that he is teaching them a far more important lesson than that he can provide bread for the body. He is driving home the lesson of the centrality of the spiritual. That is, there is a spiritual hunger in our lives as well as a physical, and there is a spiritual bread which feeds it. And without this, life would surely fail.

Jesus himself demonstrates this for us in his experience of being tempted by the devil in the wilderness. Do you remember what he said? "Man shall not live by bread alone . . ." That is not enough for your humanity. If all you are interested in is food and shelter and luxuries—the visible things of life—your humanity is going to shrivel, become weak and subject to all kinds of attacks and destructive forces. "Your spirit must be fed," Jesus said. And in the lesson of the feeding of the five thousand he made it very clear. He told them, "I am the bread sent down from heaven." If you want to keep your spirit strong so that you are able to understand what is happening to you and cope with the problems which arise out of what is happening to you, you must learn to feed upon the Lord Jesus. You must learn to take from him the strength you need—worship him, rejoice in him, and be thankful to him. And you need this every day, just as you need bread for your body.

Many times I have tried to help people who were struggling with various problems in their personal life or in their marriage. As we have talked these problems through, they have come to understand that the reason they got into the mess they did was because they had lost their perspective, had begun to see things out of focus. They could not analyze or explain what was happening to them. So they reacted wrongly and created tragedy. As we talked, they began to see this. And in prayer and the reading of the Word they began to understand again that they needed to forgive and heal and draw together. They themselves would often say they recognized the problem was that they had not maintained a spiritual relationship with the Lord. Then I have seen them go back and do well for a while, but then begin to fade again until they end up in the same mess once again. You cannot keep your spirit strong if you do not feed it. This is the lesson of this whole account here, and this is what the disciples were expected to know.

Stepping Out of Mystery

One final lesson our Lord was seeking to drive home to them was the sufficiency of the resource. This is implied in the fact that seven baskets of pieces were left over—seven hampers, the term is, large baskets full of fragments. At the close of the feeding of the five thousand there were twelve baskets left over —not the same kind of baskets, but smaller ones. As we saw in that account, twelve is the number used in Scripture to symbolize Israel, the twelve tribes of Israel. Our Lord was telling the disciples that was a truth which applied to Israel. But now he uses the number seven. Seven is the number which always implies the full manifestation of God—God in his completeness, in his fullness. This is why the number seven appears so often in the Book of Revelation, because there God is manifesting himself, stepping out of the mystery of his being into full revelation before all of his creation.

What Jesus is saying here is, "If you want to know God this way, if your heart hungers (as Paul's did—'. . . that I may know him and the power of his resurrection, and may share his sufferings, becoming like him in his death') the way to know him is to learn to feed upon him in daily satisfaction of your heart's need and to reckon upon him." This involves the Word of God: "Man shall not live by bread alone, but by every word that proceeds from the mouth of God." And then it means believing this Word, rejoicing in the One who gives it. This is feeding upon Christ.

Did these disciples learn this lesson? Unfortunately, they didn't. They were just like us. The account tells us what happened:

And he sent them away; and immediately he got into the boat with his disciples, and went to the district of Dalmanutha.

Dalmanutha is across the lake, on the western side, near the present city of Tiberias.

The Pharisees came and began to argue with him, seeking from him a sign from heaven, to test him. And he sighed deeply in his spirit, and said, "Why does this generation seek a sign? Truly, I say to you, no sign shall be given to this generation" (Mk. 8:10–12).

What shall we make of this invasion of his ministry by the Pharisees again? It is obvious that they are totally blinded men. Here they come and ask him for a sign—after they themselves had seen hundreds of signs he had done. But they are determined not to believe him. And yet, to disguise this fact by an apparent eagerness to know more of his ministry, they demand this sign. Now, it is true that the Old Testament says that any prophet must give a sign to people to prove he is indeed a prophet. We need to know this today. When prophets speak, there ought to be some sign that they are from God. In the Old Testament the sign was that they could predict something which was going to happen in the near future, and it would be fulfilled exactly as predicted. Those whose predictions are not accurately fulfilled are giving clear evidence that they are not prophets from God.

But our Lord refused to give any sign because he knew these men. He knew their hardened hearts, knew that they were beyond belief in a sign. Matthew says that he added the words, "An evil and adulterous generation seeks for a sign; but no sign shall be given to it except the sign of the prophet Jonah. For as Jonah was three days and three nights in the belly of the whale, so will the Son of man be three days and three nights in the heart of the earth." That is, the only sign that would be given them was the sign of the resurrection. Yet it is true that when the resurrection did occur, these Pharisees did not believe even this sign. So no sign would be given to them now. Jesus refused to work a miracle. Leaving them in their blindness and stubborn determination to unbelief, he departed:

> And he left them, and getting into the boat again he departed to the other side. Now they [the disciples] had forgotten to bring bread; and they had only one loaf with them in the boat. And he cautioned them, saying, "Take heed, beware of the leaven of the Pharisees and the leaven of Herod." And they discussed it with one another, saying, "We have no bread" (Mk. 8:13–16).

I do not know if you can, but I cannot understand why they said, "We have no bread," when he said, "Beware of the leaven of the Pharisees and the Herodians"—except that it indicates the workings of a bad conscience. They had forgotten to buy bread, and they thought he was rebuking them for that. The moment he mentioned leaven, which is remotely connected with bread, they tied it in, due to their bad consciences, with their failure to bring enough bread for lunch. That is how dull and confused they were, how completely they failed to understand what he was saying. It was very much like the husband who said to his wife, "Where did you get that dress?" to which she replied, "Well, it was 40 percent off!" The only connection between the question and the answer is a bad conscience. I think that was the case here.

What Produces Dullness

Our Lord had intended to warn them of what produces dullness, what produces the condition they had just witnessed with the Pharisees. What in the world makes men so incredibly blind that, when One is standing before them doing all these wonderful signs and speaking these marvelous words, they should nevertheless insist upon another sign? He was warning them of what produces the condition because they were in danger of doing the same thing themselves. He put it in these graphic terms: "Beware of the leaven of the Pharisees, and the leaven of Herod." Leaven is a picture of evil doctrine or teaching. He was saying, "The reason the Pharisees are so blind is because of what they believe, what they teach. The reason Herod cannot recognize me is because of what he believes, what he teaches."

The Pharisees believed that God was interested only in what you do, in performance. Jesus said that if this is the way you live, if you think God is concerned only with what you have accomplished, with what your activity has been on his behalf, then you are going to dull your spirit and miss all the great lessons of life he wants you to learn. It will cause you to lose out on the excitement of faith, and you will become lethargic, apathetic, dull, and listless.

Or if, like Herod, your eyes are on man and the world around and you are interested only in doing what makes you acceptable to others and not what makes you acceptable to God, that too will dull your spirit. It will lead you to become blind and foolish in the way you act. This is what he was teaching them here, and he presses on in the matter: "And being aware of it, Jesus said to them, 'Why do you discuss the fact that you have no bread?'" "Why do you do that?" he says. And then he asks a series of six very perceptive questions:

> "Do you not yet perceive or understand? Are your hearts hardened? Having eyes do you not see, and having ears do you not

hear? And do you not remember? When I broke the five loaves
for the five thousand, how many baskets full of broken pieces did
you take up?" They said to him, "Twelve." "And the seven for
the four thousand, how many baskets full of broken pieces did
you take up?" And they said to him, "Seven." And he said to
them, "Do you not yet understand?" (Mk. 8:17–21).

In this series of questions, our Lord is suggesting for them,
and for us, what to do when we get the spiritual "blahs." A
young man came up to me once and said, "I'm a graduate of a
Bible college. I've been a Christian for a number of years. But
I must tell you that I feel so blah, so empty. I've lost all interest
in what God is doing, and I just don't have any desire even to
get involved in a Bible study any more. What should I do?" I
had just been studying this passage, so I did what our Lord
suggests here, without telling this young man what I was doing.

The first thing the Lord suggests is—use your mind. "Do
you not perceive or understand?" Stop and think about where
you are, about what is happening to you and why it happened.
Analyze it. Read what the Bible has to say about it. That is
what the mind is for. Study the revelations of God to you. Use
your mind.

Second, he asks, "Are your hearts hardened?" That is, analyze
the state of your heart. Are you dull or do you respond? Have
you forgotten truth? Because if the heart does not respond to
what the mind has understood, then it is because you have not
really believed it. You may have recognized mentally that it is
true, but you have not acted upon it. You do not really believe
God is going to do what he has said he will do, that is the
problem. This is always revealed by a dull, unresponsive heart.
Truth always moves us . . . when we believe it. It always
grips us and excites us. And if we are not excited, if we do not
feel a response of joy, it is because the mind has grasped it but
the heart has not. One of the things the Word suggests we do

at this point is to pray that the eyes of our heart might be enlightened.

Jesus moves on: "Having eyes do you not see, and having ears do you not hear?" Jesus said these words again and again to the people he taught, and each time he means the same thing. Do not just look at the events you are seeing and think that is all there is to it. It is a parable, a parallel to something deeper and more important concerning your spirit. As these men were being fed by the loaves and the fishes, he was saying to them, "Don't think of this merely as a way of getting a good, quick, free meal. Remember that I am telling you that you have a deeper need, a far more demanding need, which needs daily replenishment as well. Use your eyes to see beyond the physical to the spiritual."

And finally, "Do you not remember?" Hasn't God taught you things in the past through your circumstances? Hasn't he led you through events which have made you understand something about your life? Do you think that the things happening to you right now, whoever and wherever you are, are just accidents? Or is God saying something to you? Do you not remember the times he said things like that in the past? Well, remember them now, interpret these events now, and recognize that you are in the hands of a loving Father who has put you right where you are to teach you a very needed truth. Learn to lay hold of that truth and rejoice!

This is the way to keep spiritually alive and alert, vital, and functioning as a believer. That is what Jesus taught these men. And the question now hangs over each one of us. "Do you not yet understand?"

14

The Turning Point

The passage we come to now involves one of the strangest and most remarkable miracles of Jesus. It is the only one he ever performed in two stages, the only one which involved a process instead of immediate healing. Mark is the only one who records this miracle for us, and for that reason it is rather obscure. Nevertheless, it is a very significant miracle, and it has direct bearing on the startling change in the message of Jesus which follows this incident. This account brings us to the turning point in the Book of Mark—the place where the message of Jesus takes a new direction. It marks the halfway point in the teaching of this book. I hope it may be the turning point in your life as well. Let us look together now at Mark 8, beginning with verse 22:

And they came to Bethsaida. And some people brought to him a blind man, and begged him to touch him. And he took the blind man by the hand, and led him out of the village; and when he had spit on his eyes and laid his hands upon him, he asked him, "Do you see anything?" And he looked up and said, "I see men; but they look like trees, walking." Then again he laid his hands upon his eyes; and he looked intently and was restored, and saw everything clearly (Mk. 8:22–25).

Two things are of particular interest in this account. One is the process our Lord followed in this healing, and the other is the prohibition he imposed on this man. The process is unique. No other miracle is like this one. In a sense that is not strange because Jesus never did two miracles alike. We tend to fall into patterns and habits, and any change takes us by surprise. But our Lord was not that way. He did things according to what the situation demanded, and so no two miracles are really the same. But this one is very remarkably different, because of two unusual aspects.

Symbolic Spit

The first that captures our attention is that he spit on the eyes of this man. This may seem unhygienic to some of us, but in three of our Lord's miracles he employed spit in this way. In the healing of the man who was deaf and dumb, Jesus spit upon his own fingers before he touched the man's tongue. And in John's Gospel we have the account of the healing of the man who was born blind. There Jesus spit on the ground, mixed clay with it, and used that to anoint his eyes. Now he spits directly on the eyes of this blind man.

It is difficult to know exactly why. Many of the commentators have wrestled with this problem. William Barclay suggests that this was done as an accommodation to the people's belief that there is something therapeutic about human saliva. People do immediately put to their mouth a finger that is cut or burned to soothe it. That may well be where this belief arose, and there may be some weight to the suggestion. But it does not explain fully what our Lord was doing.

It seems to me—and you can regard this as a Stedmanac version, if you like—that what our Lord does is symbolic, as were all of our Lord's miracles. They were parables in action, pictures of the truth he was attempting to convey. And in this case, spit becomes a symbol of the Word of God. Spit comes from the mouth, as do our words. Thus, spit symbolizes the Word. It is the Word which is the creative agency in God's work, always. The author of the letter to the Hebrews tells us that we understand it is by the Word of God that the worlds were framed out of things which do not appear. This is what I believe is symbolized here.

The second unusual aspect of this miracle is the incompleteness of the healing. We have no other account in Scripture of anything like this, of there being a process involved in our Lord's healings. In every other circumstance he spoke the word, and instantly the person was made whole. He leaped, if he were lame; opened his eyes and saw, if he were blind; or rose from the dead. But for this miracle alone a two-stage process was involved. Again, many have wondered about this. Some commentators suggest that this represents a weakening of Jesus' powers, that he had reached a stage in his ministry where opposition was so intense, hostility so increased, that his power was not quite adequate and it took a double dose in order to accomplish the healing.

I cannot subscribe to that "double-whammy" school of thought. Our Lord always had adequate power to deal with any situation because, as he tells us so frequently himself, it was not his power; it was the power of God the Father at work in him. And, again and again through the pages of the Scriptures God teaches us that nothing is impossible to him. It was thus he challenged the faith of Sarah, the wife of Abraham, when he told them she would have a child, after her body had long since passed the age of childbearing. Sarah laughed in disbelief. And God said to her, "Is anything too hard for God?"

Some commentators have suggested that perhaps this was a very stubborn case of blindness here, much more difficult than the usual. But that is saying the same thing—that Jesus' power was not adequate to deal with it.

Rather, we must see this as a deliberate act done for the benefit of the disciples. Jesus is teaching them again by what he does and what he says. Here he deliberately does this in a two-stage fashion because he wants these disciples to see that *they* are like this blind man—they, and we who read this account—and that they need their eyes opened in two stages, as this blind man did. Therefore, this miracle is symbolic of the developments which follow this account. If we read it this way, we will see it as a very accurate introduction to what follows.

But before we continue, look briefly at the prohibition our Lord laid upon this man: "And he sent him away to his home, saying, 'Do not even enter the village' " (Mk. 8:26).

The village was Bethsaida. Our Lord had done many miracles there. But now he keeps the man from entering. This surely is in line with what we have seen many times. Jesus did not want to encourage the love of the miraculous which was so easily awakened among these people, as it still is in our own day. He *did* heal physically and there *were* miracles, but he was never happy with the reaction of those who simply wanted to see miracles. Now he exerts an even stricter control. He will not even let the man go into the village, lest the man should break his charge, as others had done before him, and tell what Jesus said he should not tell. So he limits this man in order to play the miracle down, for he always sought to strike at the real need of man—the spiritual hurt within—and to heal that.

On the Way to Mount Hermon

This is followed immediately by the account of the questions our Lord put to his disciples on the way to Caesarea Philippi, beginning at verse 27:

And Jesus went on with his disciples, to the villages of Caesarea Philippi; and on the way he asked his disciples, "Who do men say that I am?" And they told him, "John the Baptist; and others say, Elijah; and others one of the prophets." And he asked them,

"But who do you say that I am?" Peter answered him, "You are the Christ." And he charged them to tell no one about him (Mk. 8:27–30).

We must take due note of what Mark tells us here as to the location of this event. It was on the way to Caesarea Philippi. This was in the northern part of the Holy Land, north of the sea of Galilee, at the foot of Mount Hermon. It is evident that our Lord was on his way to Mount Hermon, deliberately, in order that the Transfiguration (which follows immediately) might take place on that high mountain. He understood that this was about to happen. He knew he was to be transfigured before several of these men. We must link this, then, with the transfiguration of Jesus on the mountaintop.

On the way, Mark tells us, he asked two questions of the disciples: one concerning the view of the people regarding himself, and the other concerning the disciples' own view of him. The question concerning the view of the people elicited the answer that some people thought he was John the Baptist, risen from the dead. Others thought he was Elijah the prophet, because there are Scripture references in the Old Testament which say Elijah is to come before the great and terrible day of the Lord, and they were looking for him. It is still true today in orthodox Jewish ceremonies that a chair is set out for Elijah at the Passover feast. So some said, "This is Elijah; he has arrived." And some said, "No, he is one of the other prophets—Jeremiah, perhaps, or Isaiah." Or perhaps some meant when they said, "He is one of the prophets," that they thought he was a new member of the great line of Hebrew prophets.

The people were saying these same things about Jesus back in chapter 6, where Mark records how aroused Herod the king was because of this stirring popular movement. So it is evident that the view of the multitude had not changed in these intervening eight months of ministry. They still thought he was one of the great Hebrew prophets. This indicates that they held him in very high regard, for these were the great names of Israel. But never once is it recorded that the populace had even the slightest inkling that this is the Messiah. They thought of him as one who was looking for another yet to come, and there is no indication that they ever got beyond that view.

No Reincarnation

Before we leave this, I would like to make one peripheral observation. Notice that the expectation of the multitude was not centered in what is today called "reincarnation." We hear a great deal about reincarnation these days. Many feel that the Scriptures teach reincarnation, but such is not the case. These people were not suggesting a reincarnation when they said, "He's Elijah, or John the Baptist, or Jeremiah." Reincarnation means appearing in a new body, or even as a different form of life, and leading a different life than the one originally led. We sometimes hear startling accounts of people who have been taken back by some kind of hypnotic trance into a "previous existence," in which perhaps they were of a different sex, even, and who recount all kinds of strange things happening to them. Many people, even Christians, are misled by this and think that the Scriptures suggest this may be true. Some have claimed that a passage such as this supports the doctrine of reincarnation.

There is absolutely nothing at all in Scripture that ever supports the notion of reincarnation. In this case it was not a matter of the people's thinking the old prophets had appeared in a new form. They thought it was the same old prophets back again—not a reincarnation, but the reappearance they were expecting of the same individuals who had lived hundreds of years before. Reincarnation, I make bold to say, is one of those "doctrines of demons" Paul speaks of, taught by lying spirits who deceive men and make them believe this kind of thing in order to gain control over them.

But let us go on to the question Jesus asked the disciples

themselves. He said to them, "But who do *you* say that I am?"
That was the important question to him. Peter's reply is immediate and definite: "You are Messiah, the Christ." We need
to remember that the word "Christ" is simply the Greek form
of the Hebrew word "Messiah"; they mean exactly the same
thing. It is not a name, but a title. Many people seem to think
that Jesus was his first name and Christ was his last name—like
John Smith. But Christ is not a name. Christ is the title of the
office he holds. Jesus is his name; Christ is his office. And, in
either the Greek or the Hebrew form, it means "The Anointed
One," the One anointed by God. In the Old Testament there
were two offices which required anointing: king and priest.
When Peter answered with the words, "You are Messiah, the
Christ, (the Anointed One)," he meant, "You are the One
whom God has anointed King. You are the King, the coming
One predicted of old to rule over the people of God and over
the nations of earth. You are also the Priest who is coming, the
Anointing One."

Matthew records that Jesus said immediately to Peter, "Flesh
and blood has not revealed this to you." That is, "You did not
come to this by simply reasoning it out, by normal human
methods. Rather, it was revealed to you by my Father who is
in heaven." Our Lord recognized that these disciples were being
taught by the Holy Spirit, that as they read the Scriptures, saw
the things that were happening, and observed what he was
doing, their eyes were being opened to the significance of these
events by the Holy Spirit. This teaching ministry of the Spirit is
still going on.

We must link this with the account in chapter 4 of the stilling of the storm eight months before when the disciples said to
themselves, *"Who* then is this, that even the wind and the
waves obey him?" That question needed to be answered. And
all the intervening events which followed were used by our
Lord as teaching situations that he might instruct these disciples
as to who he was. Now the test has come: he asks them the

question, "Who do you say that I am?" Peter's answer was clear and sure: "You are the Christ. You are the One we have been looking for. You are not Elijah; you are not Jeremiah, or John the Baptist. You are not one who is looking for another; you are the Other for whom all men have been looking." It must have been a startling realization to these disciples that here indeed was the One of whom all the Old Testament Scriptures spoke. Peter expressed their faith—they had arrived at it that very moment—when he said those words: "You are the Christ." Now, this is what Jesus wanted them to know. He had been working with them toward this end. He knew they needed to come to this knowledge, and all he had done up to that point had been designed to lead them to this understanding of who he was in order that they might then answer their own question.

The First Touch

But now, once they know, he does a strange thing. Mark tells us he *charged* them, laid it on them heavily, to tell *no one* about it. Is that not strange? Would you not think, now that he has brought them to this place and they know who he is, that this would be the time he would say to them, "Now I want to send you out again. Go into every village and hamlet in Galilee and tell them who I am. This is why I have come, that men might understand"? But instead, he lays it upon them not to tell anyone what they have just learned. This is one of the puzzling developments in the ministry of Jesus. And yet we can see why he did this in the light of the story of the blind man just preceding. This is that first touch which opened their eyes to a part of the truth. They saw him, but not clearly. They saw him "as a tree, walking." They saw his greatness and his glory. But they did not understand the secret of it. They still require the second touch, and this is what our Lord goes on to give.

Looking back on this now, we can see how wise his actions

were. The disciples, at this point, had great misapprehensions as to what the kingdom of God was like. And though they had come to a recognition of who he was, they had no idea how he was going to accomplish his work. They were astounded by him—amazed and dazzled and fascinated—but uncomprehending of what he really was like. They did not see him very clearly.

I once heard Major Ian Thomas give a series of splendid messages on the person of our Lord. He was commenting on this scene and the one that follows—the Transfiguration. I remember him saying that if the disciples had gone out now to tell what they knew about Jesus, if they had spread the word all over the land that here was the One the Old Testament had predicted was coming—with their superficial and shallow concepts of what this involved—they would have created a tremendous emotional reaction among the people, a popular following after Jesus, but one based upon very inconclusive and incomplete evidence. Major Thomas said that undoubtedly they would have stirred up the people to such a degree that all over Israel you would have seen donkeys with little stickers on their tails which said, "Snort if you love Jesus"!

No More Riddles

Well, I am not sure that is what would have happened, but it does indicate how little these disciples really understood of him, even though they knew he was the Christ. So our Lord moves immediately, as with the blind man, to a second touch.

And he began to teach them that the Son of man must suffer many things, and be rejected by the elders and the chief priests and the scribes, and be killed, and after three days rise again. And he said this plainly. And Peter took him, and began to rebuke him. But turning and seeing his disciples, he rebuked Peter, and said, "Get behind me, Satan! For you are not on the side of God, but of men" (Mk. 8:31–33).

I am sure Peter expected to be commended for this. Matthew tells us that our Lord *did* commend him for saying, "You are the Christ." But then our Lord had begun to do a strange thing in these disciples' eyes: he described to them the death that would come. This is what Paul later calls "the word of the cross." You notice that both Matthew and Mark specifically tell us that it was at this point that he *began* to teach them about the cross. He had hinted at it before. There are several accounts of it in the Gospels before this. The event, of course, was known to the Lord from the very beginning. In John's Gospel we are told that in his earliest ministry in Jerusalem Jesus said to the Jews, "Destroy this temple, and in three days I will raise it up again." He had said to Nicodemus, who came to him by night, "The Son of man must be lifted up, even as Moses lifted up the serpent in the wilderness." He had said to these disciples, "The friends of the bridegroom will fast when the bridegroom is taken away." And just a few days earlier, as Matthew records, he had said there would be given the sign of the prophet Jonah: "As Jonah was three days and three nights in the belly of the whale, so will the Son of man be three days and three nights in the heart of the earth." But these allusions were in the nature of riddles, and the disciples did not understand them.

But now Jesus began plainly to *declare* this. The tense of the Greek verb in verse 32 is such that it should be translated, "he continued saying this plainly." Over the course of several days, perhaps, he taught them what would happen. He named the enemies they would face when they came to Jerusalem—the chief priests, the scribes, the Pharisees—and described what they would do to him. Other accounts tell us that he detailed this: the scourgings and beatings, and the rejection that would be involved. He plainly told them all that was going to happen.

I do not think Peter's reaction was immediate. Evidently, after several days of listening to Jesus talking this way, finally he could stand it no longer. Speaking for all the disciples, he took Jesus aside and rebuked him. Imagine—Peter rebuking

Jesus! He said, "Lord, you mustn't talk this way. Why, this is terrible!" What he literally said was, "Spare yourself."

We can understand how he felt, I hope. Imagine what the reaction would be here in the United States if, on his inauguration, a popular young President detailed for this nation all the things he hoped to accomplish in his administration, injected a new note of hope among the people, and captivated us all by what looked like a tremendously successful program he intended to launch, but then, at the close, announced that he was suffering from terminal cancer and would be dead within a week. Can you imagine the reaction? People would be astounded, shocked, incredulous: "How can he even hope to accomplish what he has outlined, if that is the case?" This is the reaction of the disciples here. They find his words unbelievable. They are startled, amazed, mystified. So finally Peter rebukes the Lord.

A Familiar Voice

And in that rebuke of Peter, according to the words Matthew gives us, you find the basic philosophy of the world stated very precisely: "Spare yourself. Spare yourself, Lord! Nothing is more important than you." Is this not the way men live? "I'll give up anything except my own interests. Nothing is more important than I am." And when Peter uttered these words, Jesus said, "Get behind me, Satan! You're an offense to me, for you do not understand the things of God, but of men." This is the way men live. We all feel the pressure of this philosophy upon us. "Think of yourself first. Take care of yourself. Provide for yourself—nobody else is going to do it." How that attitude underlies everything we see on television, in magazines, and all the other media. The whole advertising system of our day is built upon it. "You deserve the best. You deserve this vacation. You deserve all that we are offering to you. Think of yourself." But Jesus said this is Satan—offering that which leads to despair and emptiness and death even though it *seems* to offer fulfillment and satisfaction. And so he rebukes Peter in turn with this stern rebuke, withering in its directness and bluntness: "Get behind me, Satan! I recognize that voice. It came to me in the temptation in the wilderness. 'There's another way to get all that God wants for you. Think of yourself.' "

I want to set before us what the word of the cross really is, the elements which make it up. For this is what the Apostle Paul tells us is the glory of the Christian message: "But far be it from me to glory except in the cross of our Lord Jesus Christ, by which the world has been crucified to me, and I to the world" (Gal. 6:14).

Christianity without the cross is not Christianity at all, but a shabby, slimy substitute. The word of the cross is what makes it Christian. What does it mean? That word contains three elements, which are found all through the Gospels and the Epistles as well. First, it means the end of the natural, the end of what we call "self-sufficiency," "self-reliance." That is the philosophy of the day, and how the world despises this message that it must be done away with! Not only does it not understand it, it literally despises it! Anyone who preaches it is regarded as preaching nonsense. As Christians, we are called upon either to believe our Lord or the voices that whisper in our ears —one or the other. Which is right? The word of the cross means the end of all reliance upon ourselves. As the little jingle puts it,

> Your best resolutions must wholly be waived,
> Your highest ambitions be crossed.
> You need never think that you'll ever be saved
> Until you have learned that you're lost.

Somehow there lingers in each one of us a desire to have a part in our salvation, to offer something to God that he can use and that he would not have if we did not give it to him, i.e., to make God our debtor in some degree. But the cross ends all

that, wipes out everything that is of the natural. Nothing that
we have by virtue of being born is ever worthwhile or acceptable in the sight of God. A cross wipes a man out. It does
not improve him, does not better him in any way; it wipes him
out. It does not send him out to be reoriented; it cuts him clear
off.

Reduced to Ashes

Furthermore, the second element is that it involves pain and
hurt. It always does, because we do not like being cut off. That
is why people do not like some of the words of the old hymns.
Sometimes I hear Christians saying, "I don't like to sing those
old hymns that talk about how *vile* and *full of sin* I am." Or,
"Amazing grace, how sweet the sound, that saved a *wretch* like
me." People say, "I'm not a wretch; I'm not vile and full of
sin!" That means, of course, that they have never stood before
the greatness and the glory of God and seen themselves as did
Job, who said, "I repent in dust and ashes." But that is what the
cross does, and it hurts. It means all our trust in ourselves is
reduced to nothing, to ashes.

Which of us, if allowed to choose the program by which we
serve God, would ever include in it defeat and disaster, despair
and disappointment, disillusionment and death? Yet these are
the very elements, the Scriptures tell us, that God finds absolutely essential to working out his plan for us, his redemptive
program. Difficulty, and danger? Yes, we would put them in;
they challenge the flesh and make it appear to be worth something when it surmounts these. But defeat? Never! Dishonor?
Never! Disaster? Disappointment? No! Death? Inconceivable!
But they are what God chooses. And so the way of the cross
always hurts, causes pain, brings us to the end of ourselves.

Jesus put it precisely when he said, "That which is highly
esteemed among men is abomination in the sight of God."
What is highly esteemed among men? Prestige and status, success, wealth and money, influence and fame and power. They,

Jesus says, are abomination in the sight of God. His standard of values is entirely different. The cross is the most radical idea ever to come into human knowledge. We have never understood Christianity until we have understood the cross. Like these disciples, we have never seen Jesus until we have seen him as one who was headed toward a cross. So our Lord begins to touch their eyes again that they might see him as he really is.

But the third element of the way of the cross, one that is always included, is that it leads to a resurrection. Is it not strange that the disciples never seemed to hear Jesus when, every time he spoke of the cross, he said that after three days he would rise again? It never dawned on them what that meant. Never did they get to that point. They seemed arrested by the cross and could never get beyond it. They rejected it, refused to listen to it, and so they never came to an understanding of what the glorious event of the resurrection would mean until it actually happened. They never asked Jesus about it, never questioned him as to what it would mean. But the way of the cross always leads to a resurrection, to a new beginning on different terms. It leads to freedom, to being set free from natural catastrophe and disaster, to having your spirit peaceful and at rest, despite what is happening to your body or your person. That is what a resurrection provides—a new beginning on entirely different terms.

This is what men really want. How we long for and dream of being free, whole, wholesome people—adequate, able to handle life, able to cope with whatever comes, undisturbed at heart. But how can we get there? How can we make our dream become reality? By the very thing we do not like to hear: the announcement of Jesus that it must be by way of the cross.

We need a second touch, don't we? We all struggle with this. Every Christian must be taught this by the Spirit of God. Jesus himself said there would be these two stages: "Come to me, all who labor and are heavy laden, and I will give you rest." There you learn who he is, in the fullness of his power to give rest to a struggling, weary, laden heart. Ah, but that is not all: "Take my yoke upon you, and learn from me; for I am gentle and lowly in heart [having lost all pride, all prestige and status], and you will find rest for your souls." Two stages. That is what our Lord has illustrated for us in this healing of the blind man, and now he begins to bring into our knowledge the second stage, by which we will understand and see clearly who he is.

15

The Way of the Cross

We have been watching One who came as the servant of man—healing, helping, comforting, restoring—yet with such power and authority that, along with the disciples, our eyes have been opened finally to see that he is nothing less than the Lord of glory himself, that he is "The Servant Who Rules" in all the far-flung creation of God. This has been the theme of the first half of our study in Mark.

But no sooner have we discovered who Jesus was and is, than, incredibly, he begins to speak about his death. This was startling to the disciples, and it represents the turning point in the Gospel of Mark. From this point, Jesus is on his way to Jerusalem, to the darkness of Gethsemane's garden, to the judgment hall of Pilate, to the whipping post, and to the bloody cross. Yet on the way, he is still ministering to men, still healing, still comforting, still cleansing, restoring, and blessing men, but now he is "The Ruler Who Serves." This chapter is both an end and a beginning. With it we have come to the end of the first half of Mark's Gospel and of Jesus' teaching concerning his identity. It is the beginning, though, of our Lord's preparation of his disciples for the dire event that awaits him as he comes into Jerusalem. The second half of our study in Mark is contained in a separate book entitled *The Ruler Who Serves.*

Now we continue with that part of Jesus' preparation of the disciples which took place at Caesarea Philippi, in the north of Galilee at the foot of Mount Hermon. After Jesus had announced the cross to his disciples, had been rebuked by Peter, and had rebuked him in turn, Mark tells us,

> And he called to him the multitude with his disciples, and said to them, "If any man would come after me, let him deny himself and take up his cross and follow me" (Mk. 8:34).

This is our Lord's outline of the process of discipleship. Here, in his own words, we look at what it means to be a disciple. The very fact that our Lord called the multitudes together *with* the disciples has raised questions in people's minds. Many have wondered if this indicates that he was seeking to make disciples, i.e., evangelizing; or was he simply telling his own disciples what it will mean to live as disciples? In other words, can you be a Christian and not be a disciple? Is discipleship a second stage of Christianity? Are there many Christians, but only relatively few disciples? *Can* you be a Christian and not be a disciple? This is a very important question, and one our Lord himself will answer for us.

Let us focus our attention now on these simple but very crucial words of Jesus, whereby he gives us the process of discipleship. There are three steps, he says. First, "If any man [anyone] would come after me, let him deny himself . . ." Notice that he does not say, "Let him hate himself." He is not asking us to deny our basic humanity, our personhood. If you take it that way, you have missed the point. And he is not telling us that we are to abandon ourselves. We cannot get outside of ourselves in any way. So we must understand what he does mean by this phrase, "deny himself," which is the first step of discipleship.

No Connections

The word "deny" means to "disavow any connection with" something, to state that you are not connected in any way with whatever is in view. Interestingly enough, it is the very word used to refer to Peter's denial of Jesus a little later on. As he was standing in the courtyard of the high priest, warming himself at a fire, a maiden asked him, "Do you know this man?" Peter denied that he had any connection with Jesus, said he did not know him, and affirmed his disavowal with oaths and curses. Thus, he denied his Lord. That is exactly the word Jesus chooses when he tells us that, if we are going to come after him, we must first deny ourselves.

It is important also to understand that he does not mean what we usually mean by "self-denial." By this we usually mean that we are giving up something. Many people feel it is only right to deny themselves something during Lent—to give up various bad habits. But Jesus is not talking about this kind of "self-denial." He is never concerned about what we *do* so much as with what we *are*. Therefore, he is not talking about giving up luxuries, or even necessities, but about denying *self*, which is entirely different. Denying *self* means that we repudiate our natural feelings about ourselves, i.e., our right to ourselves, our right to run our own lives. We are to deny that we own ourselves. We do not have the final right to decide what we are going to do or where we are going to go. When it is stated in those terms, people sense immediately that Jesus is saying something very fundamental. It strikes right at the heart of our very existence because the one thing that we, as human beings, value and covet and protect above anything else is the right to make ultimate decisions for ourselves. We refuse to be under anything or anybody but reserve the right to make the final decisions in our lives. This is what Jesus is talking about. He is not talking about giving up this or that, but about giving up ourselves. Paul says the same thing Jesus is saying: "You are not your own; you were bought with a price" (1 Cor. 6:19-20). If you are going to follow Jesus, you no longer own yourself. He has ultimate rights; he has Lordship of your life. So you no longer belong to yourself; he must make those final decisions when the great issues of your life hang in the balance. This is what Jesus means by, "If anyone would come after me, let him deny himself"—deny our self-trust, deny our self-sufficiency, deny our feeling that we are able to handle life by ourselves and run everything to suit ourselves.

Some years ago I read an article entitled, "The Art of Being a Big Shot," written by a friend of mine, a prominent Christian businessman named Howard Butt. Among many other good things he said were these words which I quote because they are so illustrative of what our Lord means here:

> It is my pride that makes me independent of God. It's appealing to me to feel that I am the master of my fate, that I run my own life, call my own shots, go it alone. But, that feeling is my basic dishonesty. I can't go it alone. I have to get help from other people, and I can't ultimately rely on myself. I'm dependent on God for my very next breath. It is dishonest of me to pretend that I'm anything but a man—small, weak, and limited. So, living independent of God is self-delusion. It is not just a matter of pride being an unfortunate little trait, and humility being an attractive little virtue; it's my inner psychological integrity that's at stake. When I am conceited, I am lying to myself about what I am. I am pretending to be God, and not man. My pride is the idolatrous worship of myself. And that is the national religion of Hell!

That is a very eloquent explanation of what Jesus means when he says, "If anyone would come after me, let him deny himself. Let him give up his rights to run his life, let him submit himself to my leadership, to my Lordship." This is fundamental to all discipleship. There can be no discipleship apart from it.

The second step immediately follows: "Let him deny himself, and take up his cross . . ." What does "take up his cross" mean? Well, I am sure these words falling on the disciples' ears were almost totally incomprehensible to them. They did not know what he meant. To them, the cross was but a very vague, hazy blur on the horizon of their minds. They did not understand where Jesus was heading. But he knew. And he knew that after the awful events which were to come in Jerusalem, after the terrible, searing pain of those days was answered by the joy and the glory of resurrection, they would think these words through again and begin to understand what he meant. We who live on this side of the cross find it easier to know what he meant.

Still, many people think that a cross is any kind of trial or hardship you are going through, or any kind of handicap you must endure—like a bossy mother-in-law or a ding-a-ling neighbor or a physical handicap. "That's my cross," we say. But that is not what Jesus means. He himself had many handicaps, many difficulties and trials which he endured before he came to his cross. So it is not merely handicap or difficulty or trial. The cross was something different. The cross stood for something in the life of Jesus connected with shame and humiliation. It was a criminal's cross on which he was hung. It was a place of degradation, where he was demeaned and debased.

Welcome the Shame

And so the cross stands forever as a symbol of those circumstances and events in our experience which humble us, expose us, offend our pride, shame us, and reveal our basic evil—that evil which Jesus described earlier: "Out of the heart of man come evil thoughts, fornication, theft, murder, adultery, coveting, wickedness, deceit, licentiousness, envy, slander, pride, and foolishness." It is the cross which brings this out. It is any circumstance, any incident which does this to us. Jesus says, if we are a disciple, we are to welcome it. That is his meaning. "Take up your cross, accept it, glory in it, cling to it, because it is something good for you. It will reduce you to the place where you will be ready to receive the gift of the grace of God." That is why the cross is so valuable to us.

This does not mean only the big things in our life; it is the little things as well. Do you feel hurt when someone forgets your name? Do you get upset when a cashier will not cash your check? Does criticism hurt, even when you know it is justified? Are you rankled when you lose at tennis or golf? All these are minor forms of the cross at work in our lives. The Lord's word is that if we are going to be a disciple, we are not to be offended by these things, we are not to get upset about them; we are to welcome them.

You can see how radical this approach to life is, how different it is from the way the world around would tell us to act. The world says, "Escape. Avoid the situation. Or if you can't avoid it, then strike back. Get angry, get even, offend in turn. Get upset about it." But the word of Jesus is, "If you're going to be my disciple, deny yourself and take up your cross."

Then the third step is, "Follow me." This really means, "Obey me." Is it not remarkable that it takes us so long to understand that if disobedience is the name of the game before we are Christians, then certainly obedience is the name of the game after we become Christians? It must be. I am amazed at people who say that they are Christians, but then blatantly, and even pridefully, acknowledge that they do not follow the Lord —do not do what he says. Now, we all struggle with this. I myself fail at this many times. Our Lord is not talking about perfection as a disciple; he is simply telling us what discipleship means, what it involves. It involves following him. It means choosing to do or say what Jesus commands us to do or say, and what he himself did, and looking to him for the power to carry it through. This is what following him means. It is what it meant to the disciples. They obeyed him, and they were taught to look to him for whatever it took to make it possible. In the feeding of the multitude, he told them to feed the crowd, and they did. But he had to supply what it took.

This is what Christianity is all about. The Christian life is following Jesus, doing what he says—like, "Love your enemy. Pray for those who hurt you. Forgive those who offend you." Those are not merely wise and helpful words; they represent a way of life our Lord is setting out before us, to which we are expected to conform even in the moment when we least feel like it. When we do not feel like obeying or forgiving or praying, he tells us to do it anyway. "Be kind to the ungrateful and the selfish." I struggle with that one. I do not want to be kind to people who are ungrateful or selfish, but that is what the Lord says to do. "Bear one another's burdens. Freely you have received, freely give." "Follow me," means obeying these and all the many, many other exhortations of Scripture.

In the original Greek, these steps are stated in the present, continuous tense. That means, "Keep on denying yourself, keep on taking up your cross, keep on following me." This is not the decision of a moment but a program for a lifetime, to be repeated again and again whenever we fall into circumstances which make these choices necessary. This is what it means to be a disciple. Discipleship is denying your right to yourself, and taking up the cross, accepting these incidents and circumstances which expose our pride and conceit, welcoming them, and then following him—doing what he says to do, looking to him for the power.

This is not always a very appealing course, is it? I am sure that it must have struck these disciples and the multitude with very solemn and serious impact. In fact, John tells us that at this point many turned and went back and followed him no more because these words seemed to them harsh and demanding. We can always be grateful that our Lord never has invited any to come after him without letting them know what would be involved. He told them straight from the shoulder what they would be getting into. And he does this with us. He is not interested in anybody's becoming a Christian or attempting to live as a Christian on false terms. He wants us to understand that this is going to shatter us, change us, make us into a different kind of person. It is bound to. If it has any meaning in our lives at all, it is going to revolutionize us utterly right to the very basic core of our being. He makes this very clear, right from the start.

And then he goes on to give us the motive which will move us in this direction: "For whoever would save his life will lose it; and whoever loses his life for my sake and the gospel's will save it" (Mk. 8:35).

That is motive enough, certainly. Who is not interested in saving his life? That is, making it worthwhile, making it complete and full and rich, worth the living. We all want that. Deep down within us, every one of us has a hunger for life and a desire to find it to the full extent of what it was designed to be. This is what Jesus is talking about. "If this is what you want," he says, "I'll tell you how to acquire it." There are two attitudes toward life which are possible, and you can have only one or the other. One is: save your life now, i.e., hoard it, clutch it, cling to it, grasp it, try to get hold of it for yourself, take care of yourself, trust yourself, see that in every situation your first and major concern is, "What's in it for me?" That is one way to live, and millions are living that way today. All of us, at one time or another, do this.

The other attitude is: lose it, i.e., fling it away, disregard what advantage there may be for you in a situation and move out in dependence upon God, careless of what may happen to you. Paul says, "I count not my life dear unto myself." Abraham obeyed God, went out on a march without a map into a land he knew not where, apparently careless of what would happen to him. And his neighbors reproached him, rebuked him for not caring about himself. This is to be a way of life, Jesus says. Trust

God, obey him, and put the responsibility for what happens on his shoulders. This is the way of life Jesus offers—to lose your life like that.

Fundamental Law

And he says there are only two results which can follow. If you save your life, if you cling to it, hoard it, get all you can for yourself, then, without a doubt, Jesus says, you will lose it. This is not a mere platitude, a truism: he is stating a fundamental law of life. It is absolutely unbreakable. Nobody can break this law. If you save your life, says Jesus, you will lose it. You will find that you have everything you want, but you will not want anything you have. You will find that the life you tried to grasp has slipped through your fingers and you have ended up with a handful of cobwebs and ashes, dissatisfied, hollow, and empty, mocked by what you hoped to get.

There are many who are proving this today. Ask the man who has everything, "Are you happy?" He may answer, "Yes, I am. I've got everything I want; I can do anything I like; I can go anywhere, at any time. I've got all the money I need. Yes I'm happy." But if you press him, "Does that mean you're satisfied with yourself, content with your life, fulfilled, convinced that your life has been worthwhile, and that you can go to your grave with a deep sense of having invested your life well?" If you press, you will ultimately get the answer, "No, something's missing. I thought these things would fulfill me, I thought they'd satisfy that deep craving down inside, but they haven't. It is still there. I still feel there must be something beyond, something more that I haven't got." This is what Jesus is talking about. "Save your life, and you will lose it."

"But lose your life for my sake and the gospel's," says Jesus. "Lose your life by means of giving yourself away in the cause of Christ, giving up your right to yourself, taking up your cross and following me, and you will save it." You will not waste it, but you will save it. You will find a contentment and satisfaction, an inner peace, and a sense of worth about your living. You will discover, not just in heaven some day but right now, that even though you may not have all the things others have, your life will be rich and rewarding and satisfying.

There is an illustration I often use to point up this truth. I often imagine the scene when the Apostle Paul appeared before Nero, the Roman emperor, to give answer to the charges against him. There is the emperor, in his royal robes, seated upon a throne. His name was known throughout the empire. But nobody knew of Paul, this obscure little Jew, bald-headed, big-nosed, bandy-legged, totally unimpressive in his physical appearance—he says so himself in his letters. And he was a leader of an obscure, heretical little sect that was known only as troublemakers. Nobody had heard of Paul, while everybody had heard of Nero. But the interesting thing is that now, two thousand years later, we name our sons Paul, and our dogs Nero.

This is God's part in the work of discipleship. Jesus did not come to call us to ultimate barrenness, weakness, darkness, and death; he called us to life, to richness, to enjoyment, to fulfillment. But he has told us that the way there means death. Discipleship ends in life, not in death. It ends in fulfillment and satisfaction. But the only way that we can find it is by means of a cross.

Profit and Loss

The final issue is set forth in our Lord's words in the closing part of this paragraph:

"For what does it profit a man, to gain the whole world and forfeit his life ["soul" is the Greek word]? For what can a man give in return for his life [soul]?" (Mk. 8:36–37).

Oh, these questions of Jesus—how they search us! What does it profit a man to gain the whole world and lose his own life?

This question hangs over our whole generation, as it has hung over every generation since that day. What good is it to get all the things you want and have nothing with which to enjoy them, having lost your life in the process? Is it not the very essence of wisdom, if you are going to invest time and money and everything you have to make sure you are able to enjoy the result when you are through? Would anybody knowingly build a house contrary to all the zoning ordinances and building codes with the certain result that when he has spent all his money and built the house, he will not be permitted even to move in? What foolishness that would be! And yet how many lives are being built without any consideration of this question or any dealing with the God who stands at the end of the road? This is why Jesus asks, "What would it profit a man, to gain the whole world and lose his life? What can a man give in return for his life?"

Many years ago archeologists discovered the tomb of Charlemagne, the great king and emperor of France. When the tomb was opened after being closed for centuries, the men who entered it found something amazing. They found certain treasures of the kingdom, of course. But in the center of the large vault was a throne, and seated on the throne was the skeleton of Charlemagne with an open Bible on his lap and a bony finger pointing at the words, "For what shall it profit a man, if he shall gain the whole world and lose his own soul?" What a tremendous lesson from history to those of us who follow!

Jesus not only asks this question, but he also points out that there is no way we can cheat:

> "For whoever is ashamed of me and of my words in this adulterous and sinful generation, of him will the Son of man also be ashamed, when he comes in the glory of his Father with the holy angels" (Mk. 8:38).

That is, deeds and not words will tell the story. It is not what we have said we believe; it is how we have acted that will make the difference. Somebody once asked me, "What does it mean, to be ashamed of Jesus? My son, who is in high school, said to me the other day, 'You know, Dad, I've learned a way of saying grace before I eat in the cafeteria so that nobody knows about it. I just bend over and tie my shoe.' Is that being ashamed of Christ?" Yes, it is, in a way. But I do not think little incidents like this are what our Lord is talking about. We are all tempted, at times, to be nervous about professing to be a Christian or to manifest it in certain circles. And the temptation is not wrong. What our Lord is talking about here is a settled way of life which outwardly expresses conformity to Christian truth but inwardly adopts and follows and conforms to the values of the world. This, he says, is what will be revealed in that day. Remember that at the close of the Sermon on the Mount he said, "Many shall come to me in that day, and say, 'Have we not done many mighty works in your name? Have we not cast out devils, and preached in your name?' And I shall say, 'Depart from me, I never knew you, you workers of iniquity.' "

So there is the answer to the question we asked at the beginning: Can a person be a Christian and not a disciple? Well, you can come to Christ, and all who come to Christ are given life, if they mean it when they come. But it is clear that unless you take up the work of discipleship, this life is given in vain. Paul calls this "accepting the grace of God in vain." Only those who are disciples enter into an abundant life. Now, we are not all good disciples at all times; there is much of failure. And our Lord has made provision for failure in our lives. But he is talking about the heart. What is your aim? What do you really want of your life? Do you want to live it for yourself or do you want to live it for him? That is really the question.

C. S. Lewis gathers all this up very well in these words from *Mere Christianity:*

> God is going to invade this earth in force. But what is the good
> of saying you are on His side then, when you see the whole natu-

ral universe melting away like a dream, and something else—
something it never entered your head to conceive—comes crash-
ing in; something so beautiful to some of us, and so terrible to
others, that none of us will have any choice left? For this time it
will be God without disguise; something so overwhelming that
it will strike either irresistible love or irresistible horror into every
creature. It will be too late then to choose your side. There is no
use saying you choose to lie down when it has become impossible
to stand up. That will not be the time for choosing; it will be the
time when we discover which side we have really chosen, whether
we realized it before or not. Now, today, this moment, is our
chance to choose the right side. God is holding back, to give us
that chance. It will not last forever. We must take it or leave it.

This is what Jesus said to the men of his day. Becoming a
Christian is not easy. It is radical. But it is the only way to life.